How to Make Better Decisions

CRAFTED BY SKRIUWER

Copyright © 2024 by Skriuwer.

All rights reserved. No part of this book may be used or reproduced in any form whatsoever without written permission except in the case of brief quotations in critical articles or reviews.

For more information, contact : **kontakt@skriuwer.com** (www.skriuwer.com)

TABLE OF CONTENTS

CHAPTER 1: UNDERSTANDING WHAT DRIVES YOUR CHOICES

- Seeing how past experiences, beliefs, and values shape your decisions
- Noticing the role of emotions and social pressure
- Becoming more aware of hidden forces that guide your actions

CHAPTER 2: SPOTTING COMMON OBSTACLES

- Recognizing fear of failure, overthinking, and other frequent barriers
- Learning how peer pressure and unclear information create confusion
- Protecting yourself by identifying harmful triggers early

CHAPTER 3: OVERCOMING FEAR OF THE UNKNOWN

- Accepting that uncertainty is natural in life
- Breaking worst-case scenarios into manageable parts
- Building confidence by taking gradual steps into unfamiliar territory

CHAPTER 4: USING EMOTIONS WISELY

- Balancing logical thinking with healthy emotional cues
- Avoiding emotional traps like anger or overexcitement
- Turning feelings into useful signals for clear choices

CHAPTER 5: BUILDING SELF-CONFIDENCE

- Recognizing personal strengths and past successes
- Setting realistic goals and embracing small wins
- Silencing negative self-talk and trusting your ability to learn

CHAPTER 6: COPING WITH OUTSIDE PRESSURES

- Dealing with social, cultural, and family expectations
- Preserving your own voice when confronted by others' opinions
- Practicing assertive communication and boundary setting

CHAPTER 7: THINKING ABOUT POSSIBLE OUTCOMES

- Using pros and cons, scenario planning, or decision trees
- Weighing short-term gains against long-term consequences
- Spotting hidden costs or benefits in each option

CHAPTER 8: RESPONDING TO SUDDEN CHANGES

- Staying calm and flexible under unexpected pressure
- Acting quickly but thoughtfully when time is limited
- Using simple steps and support to handle urgent shifts

CHAPTER 9: ASKING FOR ADVICE AND SUPPORT

- Knowing when to seek help from friends, mentors, or experts
- Filtering conflicting advice and staying true to your goals
- Building a support network to lighten the decision load

CHAPTER 10: USING SIMPLE CHECKLISTS AND TOOLS

- Relying on checklists, calendars, and spreadsheets for clarity
- Breaking big tasks into smaller, trackable steps
- Reducing mental clutter and preventing oversights

CHAPTER 11: AVOIDING COMMON TRAPS

- Noticing pitfalls like overconfidence and the "sunk cost" trap
- Steering clear of information overload and black-and-white thinking
- Applying self-awareness to dodge repeating errors

CHAPTER 12: DEFINING CLEAR TARGETS

- *Shaping specific, measurable goals aligned with your values*
- *Breaking large aims into phased steps you can handle*
- *Regularly reviewing and adjusting targets to stay on track*

CHAPTER 13: FORMING HELPFUL ROUTINES

- *Simplifying daily life with structured habits*
- *Avoiding aimless choices by following consistent patterns*
- *Staying flexible so routines stay effective, not restrictive*

CHAPTER 14: HANDLING COMPLICATED SITUATIONS

- *Organizing multiple factors and people's viewpoints*
- *Staying calm amid high stakes and shifting details*
- *Crafting adaptive plans that can pivot when needed*

CHAPTER 15: DECIDING WHEN TO TAKE RISKS

- *Weighing potential gains against possible losses*
- *Using safety nets and small tests to manage uncertainty*
- *Turning calculated risks into opportunities for growth*

CHAPTER 16: REVIEWING WHAT WORKED AND WHAT DID NOT

- *Learning from each choice by analyzing outcomes*
- *Spotting patterns that lead to success or cause mistakes*
- *Adapting your approach through honest reflection*

CHAPTER 17: STAYING FLEXIBLE AND OPEN

- *Accepting that plans may shift with new facts or changes*
- *Balancing solid goals with readiness to adapt*
- *Letting go of rigid thinking to see better opportunities*

CHAPTER 18: FACING DOUBTS AND UNCERTAINTY

- *Understanding the roots of doubt and fear*
- *Moving forward despite incomplete information*
- *Building trust in your process to handle unknowns*

CHAPTER 19: KEEPING UP MOTIVATION

- *Finding personal meaning behind each goal*
- *Using small rewards and visual progress checks*
- *Managing energy, stress, and mindset for steady drive*

CHAPTER 20: BRINGING IT ALL TOGETHER

- *Combining self-awareness, tools, flexibility, and motivation*
- *Following a clear cycle of deciding, acting, and reviewing*
- *Carrying these methods into all areas of life to move from stuck to certain*

Chapter 1: Understanding What Drives Your Choices

When you make a choice, there are many hidden forces at work. These forces can include your thoughts, your feelings, and things you have learned over time. You might not always notice these factors, but they play a big part in deciding what you do. By understanding these forces better, you can make decisions that help you move in a direction that is good for you. This chapter will explain some basic ideas about why you make the choices you make.

---

1. The Role of Past Experiences

Your past experiences teach you how the world works. You learn what to do and what not to do based on past events. For example, if you once tried a certain ice cream flavor and did not like it, you might avoid ordering that flavor again. This might seem like a small detail, but it is a simple example of how your mind stores information. You remember what happened and try to avoid doing what caused a bad result.

Past experiences can also teach you good lessons that help you in tough moments. If you worked hard at a project and got a good grade or a positive response, you might decide to put in that same effort next time. Your past can also affect you in ways that are not so obvious. Maybe you had a disagreement with a friend once, and it made you uncomfortable, so now you feel nervous when you speak up. By paying attention to how your past influences your thinking, you can start to be more aware of why you feel a certain way about a choice. Then you can decide if that feeling is still helpful or if you should think about the situation in a new way.

---

2. The Power of Values

Values are the things that you think are important. They guide your behavior and set the tone for how you want to act in life. Some people value honesty. Others value kindness. Some might value adventure or challenge. You might value different things at different times, but often a few main values direct you most of the time.

When you make a choice, these values pop into your mind, even if you do not know it. They act like a compass that points you toward the direction that feels right. If you value honesty, you will lean toward telling the truth, even if it is hard or makes you feel uneasy. If you value kindness, you may choose to do something that helps someone else, even if it costs you some time or money. By noticing your values and naming them, you become better at seeing why you feel pulled to do some things and not others. This also helps you measure if a certain choice is good for you in the long term.

---

3. Emotional Reactions

Emotions can be strong forces that guide you in the moment. You might feel a burst of excitement, or you might feel worried when you think about a certain path. These feelings can tell you a lot about what matters to you. Fear might warn you of danger, but it can also hold you back if it is too strong. Excitement might push you to move forward, but it can also make you overlook important facts if you let it take over. The trick is to notice your emotions without letting them fully control you.

Sometimes, people think emotions are either good or bad. However, emotions are simply signals that your mind and body send you. It is helpful to look at them as hints. If something scares you, ask yourself: Is there a real danger here, or am I just feeling uncertain? If something makes you happy, ask yourself: Is this excitement enough to justify the time and effort needed? By handling emotions this way, you can use them to guide you but still keep your decisions calm and balanced.

---

4. Beliefs and Self-Talk

Everyone has beliefs about themselves and the world around them. These beliefs come from family, friends, and things learned in school or from movies and books. Some beliefs can be true and helpful, such as "I can learn if I try my best." Other beliefs might be limiting, such as "I am not good at this, so I should not try." The way you talk to yourself in your head also comes from your beliefs. You might think, "I can solve this problem," or you might think, "I will never figure this out."

When you are about to make a choice, your beliefs and self-talk shape your confidence. They affect whether you think you can handle the result of your decision. If your self-talk is positive and you believe you can find a way to succeed, you will be more likely to step forward. If your self-talk is negative, you might decide not to do something because you already believe you will fail. Recognizing these beliefs and self-talk habits is an important step if you want to change them.

---

5. Peer Influence and Social Pressure

Your family, friends, and community also affect the choices you make. Sometimes you might feel that you should choose something because everyone around you is doing it. Or you might fear being left out if you do not go along with a group. This social pressure can be harmless, like when your friends want to watch a certain movie, or it can be unhealthy, like when people push you to try something you do not feel comfortable with.

Learning to notice when you are being guided by social pressure is helpful. Ask yourself: "Am I making this choice because I want to, or because I am worried about what others will think?" This question can keep you from making choices that go against your values. It also helps you develop the skill of staying true to yourself, even if the group is pushing you in another direction.

---

6. Environmental Factors

Sometimes, your surroundings can have a bigger effect on your decisions than you might expect. Your environment includes where you live, the resources you have, and the day-to-day conditions you face. For instance, if you live in a very noisy place, you might not have the quiet you need to study or think clearly. If you have limited money, that can limit some of your choices.

However, your environment can also support good decisions. Maybe your local library offers free classes that help you learn new things. Maybe your town has parks where you can go to clear your mind. By knowing how your environment affects your choices, you can look for ways to use it for your benefit. At the same time, you can learn to manage problems that your environment might cause.

7. Desire for Quick Results

Everyone likes it when things happen fast. It can be exciting to fix a problem quickly. However, wanting fast answers all the time can push you to make decisions too quickly. You might jump at the first option that seems good, without checking if there is a better option. This habit can also keep you from seeing a longer path that might bring bigger rewards later.

When you notice you are in a hurry, pause and ask yourself if it is really worth rushing. Many good choices need some time and planning. Taking a short break to think can prevent mistakes. Remind yourself that instant answers are not always the best. By focusing on what you truly want in the long run, you can avoid choices that might bring trouble later on.

8. Habit and Routine

The choices you make often follow a pattern. You may do certain things every day without stopping to think about them because they have become habits. For example, you might always eat the same breakfast or walk the same route to work or school. Habits save you time and mental energy. However, they can also keep you stuck if you do not step back to see if they still suit you.

When deciding something new, you might lean on old habits without noticing. Ask yourself: "Am I choosing this only because I have done it before, or do I really think it is the best choice?" By being aware of your habits, you can choose to keep the ones that help you and leave behind the ones that no longer serve you.

9. Attraction to Comfort

Many people look for comfort. Making a decision that feels safe can seem easier than choosing something unknown. While comfort is not necessarily bad, it can hold you back from helpful changes. If you only pick what is familiar, you may not find new skills or experiences that can help you grow.

Learning to deal with a little discomfort can open up more possibilities. You might try something you have never done before and find that it is a good fit for you. Of course, not every new thing will be right for you, but it is better to keep the door open than to stay in the same place forever. You can check if you are simply looking for comfort by asking, "Am I saying no because it is truly a bad choice, or am I just avoiding feeling unsure?"

---

10. The Influence of Media

Today, you can see ideas everywhere: on the internet, on television, or in magazines. Advertisements might urge you to buy certain items because they promise you happiness or success. News stories might focus on certain topics and shape your view of what is important. Over time, these media messages can affect what you think is normal or desirable.

When you are trying to make a choice, it helps to be aware of how media might be affecting you. Ask yourself if you truly want something for your own reasons, or if an advertisement or social media trend put that idea in your head. By being careful, you can guard your mind against pressure that does not serve your real needs.

---

11. Reflecting on Personal Goals

An important factor that drives your choices is your goals. These might be short-term goals, like finishing a task by the end of the day, or long-term goals, like learning a new skill. Whenever you face a choice, think about how it fits with your goals. If your goal is to save money for a computer, then buying a new toy right now may not be the best idea. If your goal is to improve your health, then choosing healthy meals is more fitting than picking a meal full of sugar.

By connecting each choice to your goals, you can see the path more clearly. This process also makes it easier to say no to distractions. When you have a strong sense of what you want to achieve, your decisions become less random and more focused.

---

12. Recognizing Personal Blind Spots

Everyone has areas where they do not think as clearly as they could. You might be very good at seeing the risks in a situation, but not so good at noticing potential benefits. Or maybe you focus on benefits so much that you miss signs of danger. These are known as blind spots. They are natural, and everyone has them.

To handle these blind spots, you can seek out facts, ask others for input, or simply remind yourself to look at the parts of a situation you often ignore. Being humble about what you do not know helps you gather the right facts to make a balanced choice. By facing your blind spots, you can avoid big mistakes and become better at making decisions that help you in the long run.

---

13. The Influence of Time Pressure

Sometimes, you might be forced to make a choice quickly because of a deadline or an urgent situation. This pressure can make you stressed or even panic. Under high pressure, your mind can shift into a state where it focuses on short-term fixes rather than long-term outcomes. For instance, if you have only an hour to decide whether to accept a job, you might focus on the salary number without digging into what the job duties will be.

It is not always possible to get rid of time pressure. However, you can learn to manage it. One trick is to take a short moment to breathe and list out key points. Even if you have only a few minutes, spending half a minute on a calm check-in can help you notice details that your panicked mind might miss. This practice helps you keep a level head when time is short.

---

14. Personal Identity and Choices

Your sense of identity includes how you see yourself and the kind of person you want to be. Sometimes you might think, "I am someone who always helps others." In other cases, you might see yourself as a quiet person who likes to keep to yourself. These ideas about who you are can shape the choices you make. For example, if you see yourself as someone who stands up for what is right, you might speak out against unfairness even if it is risky.

On the other hand, your idea of who you are might also hold you back if you think, "I am not the type of person who tries that." By looking at your own identity carefully, you can figure out if it is helping you or limiting you. You have the freedom to change and grow. Realizing that your identity is not fixed can allow you to explore new choices that match who you want to be.

---

15. The Role of Health and Energy

Physical and mental health can greatly influence your ability to make a clear choice. If you are tired, hungry, or stressed, your mind will not work at its best. You might become impatient or forgetful, and that could lead to poor decisions. On the other hand, if you feel rested and calm, you can think more clearly and see possible outcomes more easily.

It is wise to notice your physical and mental state before making an important choice. If you are exhausted, try to rest or eat something healthy before deciding. If you are worried, try a short relaxation method, like taking a few slow breaths, so you can settle your mind. By taking care of your health and energy level, you give yourself the best chance to make thoughtful choices.

---

16. The Importance of Self-Awareness

Self-awareness means understanding how you think and feel at any given moment. It also means noticing how your mind reacts to different situations. When you are self-aware, you can see if you are being guided by fear or by hope. You can catch yourself if you start to let a past mistake color your current choice.

Being self-aware is something you can practice over time. One simple way is to pause once in a while and ask yourself: "How do I feel? Is this feeling helping me or holding me back?" Another way is to watch how your body feels. If your muscles are tight and your breathing is fast, you might be feeling stress. If your shoulders drop and you feel light, you might be relaxed. By tracking these signals, you get better at seeing what drives your choices in the moment.

---

17. Learning to Compare Options

When you understand what drives you, it becomes easier to compare different options. Let's say you have two options: take on a big task or focus on a smaller task. If you realize that your main value is learning, and the big task offers more learning, then that option might be a better fit for you. If your main goal is to gain rest, maybe the smaller task is better for now. The key is to line up each option with your values, your goals, and your current emotional state. This comparison helps you decide which path fits you best.

---

18. Knowing Your Limits

Everyone has limits, such as how much time they can give, how much energy they can spend, or how much stress they can handle. No matter how eager you are, you cannot do everything at once. Understanding these limits helps you make wise choices about what to take on. If you do not know your limits, you might say yes to too many things and find yourself overwhelmed.

Being aware of your limits also means you can plan better. If you know you can only handle a certain amount of work in a day, you can protect yourself from burnout by not piling on more tasks. By honoring your limits, you save energy for the choices that are truly important.

---

19. The Gradual Nature of Change

Sometimes, understanding what drives you is not enough to bring about change right away. You might know you have a habit that is not helping you, but it could take time to break it. You might see that social pressure has too big an effect on you, but learning to say no can be a slow process. Give yourself space to change step by step. Each small improvement helps you make better choices over time.

Remember that you are not stuck with your current ways of thinking. If you learn something new that shifts your perspective, it might change how you make choices. This is part of the process of growing. It can be helpful to keep track of the small steps you take. Over weeks and months, these small steps add up to bigger changes in how you decide things.

---

20. Putting It All Together

When you look at all the factors—past experiences, values, emotions, beliefs, social pressure, environment, and more—you see how complex decision-making can be. Still, it is not something to fear. By taking time to understand what drives you, you are already becoming a better decision-maker. The next chapters will help you identify common problems and figure out practical tools for clearer thinking.

The main takeaway from this chapter is that your choices are shaped by many things. You are not just one single element. You are a mix of thoughts, feelings, past lessons, personal aims, and outside influences. Understanding these elements gives you the power to see where each choice comes from. Then you can pick what works best for you in a clearer, more confident way.

Chapter 2: Spotting Common Obstacles

Making decisions is a normal part of everyday life. However, there are many obstacles that can block you from making a good decision or from making a decision at all. These obstacles can come in different forms, such as strong feelings, confusion, peer pressure, or a lack of information. If you learn to spot them early, you can prevent many of the problems that might come later. This chapter focuses on common obstacles that you might face and suggests ways to manage them.

---

1. Fear of Failure

Fear of failure is one of the biggest obstacles. Many people worry that if they choose something and it does not work, they will regret it or be embarrassed. This fear can make you so afraid of being wrong that you avoid making any move. You might say, "I will wait until I am absolutely sure," which can lead to never choosing at all.

One way to handle fear of failure is to remind yourself that failure is often a part of growth. If you do not succeed in one try, you might learn something useful for the next attempt. Also, keep your goals realistic. Instead of aiming for a huge change all at once, aim for a smaller step you are confident you can manage. By moving in smaller steps, you reduce the pressure that comes with worrying about a big mistake.

---

2. Unclear Information

Sometimes, you might feel stuck because you do not know enough to choose wisely. For example, you might need to pick a college major but not have details about job prospects. You might need to decide on medical care but not have a good understanding of the side effects. Lack of clear information can create confusion and stress.

The best way to beat this obstacle is to look for reliable facts. Ask experts or people who have experience. Read books and articles from sources you trust. If the information seems complicated, ask for help in breaking it down into simple terms. When you have enough knowledge, you can evaluate your options more confidently. Remember, it is okay to say, "I do not know yet." This means you are being careful and aiming to make a thoughtful choice.

---

3. Overthinking Small Details

Overthinking can happen when you focus too much on tiny things that might not matter in the big picture. You might read every single review of a product and still feel uncertain. You might second-guess if you should send a message at 9:00 or 9:05. Overthinking can waste time and energy, and it can even prevent you from acting at all.

To manage overthinking, try to figure out which details are truly important. Ask yourself, "Will this detail affect the outcome in a real way?" If not, let it go. It can also help to put a time limit on your decision. For instance, promise yourself you will decide by tomorrow afternoon. This pushes you to focus on what truly matters and avoid getting stuck on the small stuff.

---

4. Analysis Paralysis

Analysis paralysis is similar to overthinking, but it involves gathering more and more information without ever moving forward. You might feel like you must consider every single angle before you can be at peace with your choice. However, there is a point where more information does not give you more clarity; it only gives you more to sift through. This situation can make you stuck.

You can fight analysis paralysis by looking for a balance. Research enough so that you have a strong understanding, but then set a deadline. Tell yourself, "Once I have read five reliable articles on this topic, I will stop and decide." You can also seek guidance from someone you trust. Ask them to help you figure out what level of research is enough. Once you reach that point, take a step toward your choice and see what happens.

---

5. Focusing Only on Short-Term Comfort

Many people base their choices only on what feels good in the moment. They might ignore whether the choice helps them in the long term. This leads to decisions that bring short bursts of happiness but cause problems later. For example, spending all your savings on a fun event might be nice today, but it leaves you with no safety net if something urgent comes up tomorrow.

To avoid this obstacle, remember to check both the short-term and long-term effects of each option. Ask yourself: "How will I feel about this choice next week? Next year?" Also think about how it matches your personal aims. If a choice feels good now but hurts your long-term aim, it might not be worth it.

---

6. Being Led by Anger or Frustration

Emotions like anger or frustration can push you toward decisions that feel good in the heat of the moment but cause regret afterward. For example, you might quit a job right away because you are upset with a coworker. You might end an important friendship over a small disagreement. Making decisions while you are very upset can leave you feeling sorry later, once you calm down.

To deal with this, pause and give yourself time to cool off before you choose. If you can, take a walk, have a drink of water, or count to ten slowly. You want your mind to return to a calmer state. Then you can think through what you truly want rather than letting anger or frustration guide you. While it can be hard to wait when you are upset, it often saves you from regrettable moves.

---

7. Peer Pressure

As mentioned in the previous chapter, peer pressure can be a strong obstacle. You might want approval from a certain group, so you go along with choices that do not feel right. Or you might fear that others will judge you. Peer pressure can pull you away from your own best judgment and leave you feeling uneasy.

To manage peer pressure, keep in mind what is genuinely important to you. Try to step back from the group for a moment and think quietly. Ask yourself: "Am I agreeing with this just to fit in?" Knowing where you stand on key values makes it easier to say no when you need to. You can also rehearse polite ways of saying no, such as, "I am not comfortable with that, but thank you for including me."

8. Swayed by Appearance over Substance

Sometimes, a choice looks very attractive on the surface, but underneath it may not hold much value. For instance, you might see a cool advertisement for a new phone and feel tempted to buy it. However, after you look deeper, you might find that the phone does not meet your needs or that the price is too high. Making a choice only based on appearance can lead to disappointment once the flashiness wears off.

A helpful step is to compare what something looks like to what it can actually do. If the phone's features do not match the cost, it might not be a wise purchase. If a job offer sounds amazing but the day-to-day tasks do not match your skills or goals, it might not be a good fit. Look beyond the surface before you make a choice.

9. Unsure of Your Own Priorities

When your priorities are not clear, every option can seem equally good or equally bad. You may not know if you should focus on career or family, or if you should pick fun in the moment or plan for the future. This uncertainty can leave you feeling lost.

To clear this obstacle, take a bit of time to write down what you care about most at this point. This might mean focusing on learning a skill or making time for personal relationships. Rank your priorities. Even if it feels tough at first, having a list that shows what matters most can guide you. When you face a choice, you can compare the outcome to your top priority and see if it fits.

10. Being Unaware of Hidden Goals

Sometimes, there is a hidden reason for a choice that you might not admit to yourself. For instance, you might pretend you want a new gadget because it will help you study, but deep down you just want to show off to your friends. Or you might say you want to exercise more, but in reality you just want an excuse to avoid a chore at home. When hidden goals drive your decisions, you might find yourself feeling confused or dishonest.

A good way to spot hidden goals is to be honest about your motives. Ask yourself, "What do I truly want out of this situation?" Then check if that reason lines up with what you are telling people. You do not need to share all your motives with everyone, but being honest with yourself helps you handle obstacles better.

---

11. Getting Trapped in the Past

Some people base their choices mostly on what went wrong before. They might think, "Last time I tried this, it did not work, so I am never doing it again." While learning from past mistakes is good, letting them block you can be bad. The future is not always the same as the past. You might have grown, or the situation could be different now.

To break free from this trap, remind yourself that each new choice is its own event. Even if you made a similar choice before, the outcome could change this time if you have new skills or better resources. Also, try to focus on what you can do better now. Do not let a single past mistake keep you from trying something that might be good for you today.

---

12. Ignoring Your Own Instincts

Sometimes, you might have a strong feeling in your gut about a choice. It might be a sense of discomfort or a sense of excitement. If you ignore these instincts, you could end up picking an option that does not sit well with you. While instincts should not be your only guide, they can offer useful clues about what truly matters to you.

A balanced approach is to check your instincts against facts. If your gut says something feels wrong, try to figure out why. Is there a detail you overlooked? If your gut says something feels right, does it match what you know to be true? By giving your instincts a voice and then combining them with logic, you can avoid ignoring vital signals that your mind and body are sending you.

---

13. Negative Social Comparisons

In today's connected world, it is easy to compare yourself to others. You might see someone on social media with a certain lifestyle and feel like you should make choices that copy them. This can lead you to choose based on someone else's story rather than your own needs. Constant comparisons can also fuel feelings of envy or unhappiness.

The way to fight this is to remember that everyone's path is different. Just because a friend picked a certain career or bought a certain item does not mean it is right for you. Each of us has different goals, values, and personalities. Try to focus on what fits you instead of matching someone else.

---

14. Letting Other People Decide for You

Sometimes, you might let others make your choices just to keep the peace or to avoid blame if it goes wrong. While it can feel easier to let a friend or family member pick for you, it can rob you of control over your own life. You might also grow resentful later if their choice leads to a bad outcome.

If you see that you are about to let someone else decide for you, ask yourself if that is truly what you want. It may be helpful to hear someone's advice, but in the end, you should decide for yourself. Taking ownership of your decisions helps you grow more confident and learn from both successes and mistakes.

---

15. Feeling You Must Be Perfect

Wanting everything to be perfect is another obstacle. Perfectionists often delay making choices because they are worried the outcome will not meet their high standard. They might review every last detail or stress over small errors. While caring about quality is good, aiming for perfection can be paralyzing.

To handle this, allow some room for minor flaws. Understand that aiming for improvement is good, but perfection is not always realistic. Ask yourself if the choice meets your main requirements, rather than waiting for every tiny thing to be flawless. This mindset shift can help you take action sooner and move beyond the fear of not being perfect.

---

16. Time Constraints and Urgency

Sometimes, you might have to make a quick decision due to limited time. This urgency can be an obstacle if it makes you feel rushed. You might not have time to gather all the facts or to think about the possible outcomes. When you feel rushed, it is easy to make a choice you regret later.

Even if time is short, try to create at least a small space for calm thinking. Write down a brief list of pros and cons. If you can, ask a friend for a quick opinion. By using what little time you do have wisely, you can still come out with a reasonable decision. Urgency does not have to mean panic.

---

17. Learned Helplessness

Learned helplessness happens when a person has faced repeated problems and starts to believe they cannot change their situation. They may think, "No matter what I do, it will not work," so they give up. This attitude can keep you from even trying to make a choice that might improve your life, because you think you have no control.

If you sense you might be stuck in this mindset, look for small steps you can take to prove that you do have some control. Pick a simple choice with a high chance of success. As you see that you can cause change, you start to break out of the helplessness trap. Over time, you can build a track record of small successes that remind you you are not powerless.

---

18. Mood Swings

Some people have strong mood swings, such as feeling very happy one day and very sad the next. This can create a challenge when making decisions. If you pick an option while you are in a very good mood, you might overlook risks. If you choose while in a low mood, you might ignore the positive sides. These swings can lead to choices that do not fit what you truly need in a stable mindset.

One solution is to notice your mood and wait until it is steady if you can. If you have to choose when your mood is not stable, ask for advice from someone you trust. They might see the situation more calmly and help you keep balance in your thinking. You can also review your notes later when your mood is different to see if you still agree with your earlier thoughts.

---

19. Information Overload

In modern life, you can find endless details on almost any topic. This flood of details can be confusing. You may end up reading so many opinions that you do not know which is correct or which fits your needs. Information overload is an obstacle because it leaves you not knowing what to trust.

To manage this, learn to filter your sources. Pick a few trustworthy experts and listen to them rather than gathering views from every random person. Keep your aim in mind. If you only need to know about a certain aspect, do not read about every angle that does not relate to your situation. By focusing on the essentials, you can make the amount of information more manageable.

---

20. Physical and Mental Exhaustion

Sometimes, the main obstacle is simply being worn out. If you are exhausted from work, school, or life events, you might not have the mental energy to think clearly. This can make you skip important steps and jump to a conclusion just to get it done.

When you notice you are too tired to think properly, try to rest before deciding. Even a short break can help. If you do not have time for a full rest, do something that refreshes your mind, like stretching or taking a few deep breaths. Once you feel a bit better, you can return to the choice and see it with fresh eyes.

Chapter 3: Overcoming Fear of the Unknown

Fear of the unknown is a strong feeling that can hold people back from making choices or taking steps in life. This type of fear often appears when you are unsure what will happen next. You might be afraid of leaving your comfort zone, starting a new project, or facing a situation you have never dealt with before. Fear of the unknown can stop you from moving forward, but there are ways to manage it. In this chapter, we will explore causes of this fear and suggest helpful methods to lessen its grip on you.

---

1. **Why People Fear the Unknown**

People are wired to seek security. When you do not know how a situation will turn out, you can feel threatened. Your mind might create scary images of the worst results. Sometimes, it is not the actual event you fear, but the fact that you cannot see what is ahead. This uncertainty can make you feel out of control. In reality, no one can fully control the future, but your brain still tries to find certainty by being cautious.

Fear of the unknown may also come from past experiences. If a past new situation led to a bad outcome, you might feel anxious in new situations again. You could think, "This might go wrong, just like before." Although this reaction is meant to protect you from danger, it can also keep you from seeing positive changes that new paths might offer.

---

2. **Recognizing the Signs**

It is not always clear when you are afraid of the unknown rather than being afraid of a real threat. Some signals may include feeling tense, having racing thoughts, or wanting to delay any step that moves you into unfamiliar territory. You might also come up with excuses that allow you to stay put, such as telling yourself you are too busy or not ready yet. These excuses can be signs that fear of the unknown is working in the background.

Another clue is that you keep seeking more information, but you still feel unsettled no matter how much you learn. This endless search for knowledge can sometimes be a cover for fear. Deep down, you might think, "If I gather enough information, I can make the future certain." But no matter how much you learn, the future always has some unknown parts.

3. Breaking Down Worst-Case Scenarios

One way to handle fear of the unknown is to look at what you fear might happen. Often, your mind will imagine the worst possible results. For instance, if you are thinking about applying to a new school, you might fear you will fail the entrance exam, be rejected, and feel embarrassed. Or if you are considering a new job, you might worry that you will not fit in or that you will lose your income if you cannot do the work well.

A helpful tactic is to write down the worst-case scenarios that come to mind. Then, ask yourself how likely each one really is. Often, you will see that these extreme outcomes are not as likely as you first thought. Next, see if you could handle the worst case. You might find that even if the worst did happen, you could still manage. This exercise reduces the power that the unknown holds over you.

4. Gaining a Small Sense of Control

While you cannot remove all unknowns, you can focus on actions that give you some control. For instance, if you are scared about moving to a new city, you can plan certain parts of the move. You could research the best neighborhoods, find out about possible job openings, and note where grocery stores or public transportation are. Though this will not tell you every single thing about how your life will turn out, it gives you a foundation that reduces uncertainty.

When people feel they have some control over parts of the unknown, their fear tends to go down. Making a list of steps you can take is a good start. You do not have to figure out the entire process right away. Even just setting up one or two items you have control over can calm your mind and help you see that the unknown is not entirely out of your hands.

5. **Taking Gradual Steps**

You do not have to face the unknown all at once. Instead, try taking smaller steps. For example, if you want to move into a new field of study but are unsure if it is right for you, you might first talk to people who are already in that field. Next, you could try a short class or a volunteer project in that area. These small steps let you test the waters without making a full commitment, giving you a chance to see how you feel about it.

By taking small steps, you build a path toward the bigger change. You also gather bits of real-life data about what it might be like. Each small success can boost your confidence and reduce fear because you have proof you can handle it. Instead of jumping into a big unknown, you create a series of smaller unknowns that feel easier to handle one by one.

---

6. **Using a Support Network**

Sometimes, fear of the unknown feels bigger when you face it alone. Talking to friends, family, or mentors can help you gain fresh insights. They might have faced a similar unknown before and can share how they managed it. Even if they have not, just having someone to listen can make the fear feel less heavy.

You can also look for local groups or online communities where people discuss the type of change you are thinking about. If you are planning to start a small business, for example, joining a group of people who have done it can show you the real ups and downs, not just the scary possibilities in your head. Having support does not remove the unknown, but it can make you feel better equipped to deal with it.

---

7. **Focusing on Possible Advantages**

Fear often highlights dangers but ignores the good side of the unknown. For instance, if you are scared about switching schools, you might keep thinking about fitting in, coursework difficulty, or financial costs. However, you might also gain better opportunities, make new friends, or discover a different passion. By turning your mind toward the good things that can come from the unknown, you see that it is not all risk.

This is not about pretending risks are not real. It is about giving equal time to the positive outcomes that could happen. When you write down the possible benefits, you remind yourself that the unknown can bring good surprises as well. This balanced view can reduce fear and help you see a bigger picture.

8. Practicing Adaptability

Adaptability is the ability to handle changes without losing your footing. People who are adaptable do not try to avoid the unknown; instead, they become better at staying steady when unexpected things happen. You can practice adaptability by exposing yourself to small changes in daily life. For example, change your route to work or school one day, or try a new hobby without doing a lot of research first.

These small acts teach your mind that unfamiliar situations are not always scary. Over time, you build trust in your ability to handle whatever pops up. That trust can make bigger unknowns feel less threatening because you have taught yourself how to adjust to new things quickly.

9. Managing Thoughts That Increase Fear

The way you think about the unknown can make a big difference in how scared you feel. If you focus on thoughts like "I will not be able to handle this" or "Everything might go wrong," you feed your fear. Instead, try to replace those thoughts with more balanced ones, such as "I might face challenges, but I can find ways to handle them" or "Not everything will go perfectly, but there could be good outcomes as well."

Mindfulness exercises can help you notice when your thoughts are spinning out of control. If you find yourself stuck on scary ideas, pause and label them as "worry thoughts." Then shift your attention to something in the present moment, such as your breath or the sounds around you. This pause can break the cycle of fear and help you regain calm thinking.

10. Setting Realistic Expectations

Sometimes, fear of the unknown comes from expecting everything to be smooth and easy. If you think a new step should have no problems, you might panic when an issue appears. By setting realistic expectations, you accept that some bumps may occur. This does not mean you want problems, but it means you are not surprised if they happen.

When you plan for a possible setback, you have a strategy to handle it. For instance, if you know a new job might have a learning curve, you can give yourself extra time in the first few weeks to get used to it. This realistic view lets you walk into the unknown with less fear, because you already know that hiccups can be part of the process.

---

11. Building Confidence Through Previous Successes

Take a moment to remember times in your life when you faced something unknown but did okay in the end. Maybe it was your first day in a new school, trying out for a sports team, or starting a job you had never done before. Recall how nervous you were and how you managed to learn and adjust.

Reflecting on past successes can help you see that you have the ability to handle change. You might have forgotten those successes if you are focusing on fear right now. By bringing them back to mind, you remind yourself that the unknown did not beat you then, and it does not have to beat you now.

---

12. Accepting That Some Unknowns Cannot Be Resolved Immediately

Part of dealing with fear of the unknown is realizing that you cannot always turn the unknown into the known right away. Sometimes you have to live with a degree of uncertainty. This can be tough for people who like to plan everything in detail. However, accepting that you cannot figure it all out at once can bring relief. It frees you from fighting a battle you cannot win right now.

If you find yourself stuck in worry about an uncertain future event—like an important exam result or a job offer decision—acknowledge that you have done all you can. Once you have prepared, studied, or submitted your application, the rest might be out of your hands. Stepping back and letting the outcome unfold can save you a lot of stress.

---

13. **Keeping a Balanced View of Risk**

The unknown often involves some risk, but not every risk is huge. You can learn to weigh risk more carefully. Ask yourself what the real risk is. Are you risking a small inconvenience, or are you risking something truly major? By being honest about the size of the risk, you may find it is not as serious as you first imagined.

For instance, if you worry about speaking up in a group discussion, the risk might be that you stumble over your words or someone disagrees with you. Is that risk life-changing? Probably not. Looking at the true level of risk can show you that facing the unknown might be worth it because the actual downside is not as large as your fear suggests.

---

14. **Planning for Different Outcomes**

When you do not know how a situation will go, it can help to plan for more than one outcome. This is sometimes called "scenario planning." For each likely outcome, write what you would do next. If a certain plan works out, you will do one set of actions. If it does not, you have a backup plan. Thinking about alternative outcomes can calm fear because you see that you have options for each path.

Be sure not to overdo it. Planning for every tiny possibility can lead to overthinking. Focus on the main outcomes and come up with a basic approach for each. This balance helps you feel prepared without getting stuck in endless planning.

---

15. **Learning from Others Who Faced the Unknown**

Stories of people who overcame fear of the unknown can be inspiring. If you find people who stepped into something new and came out stronger, you see that it is possible to handle uncertainty. These do not have to be famous figures. They can be neighbors, relatives, or friends. Ask them how they felt and what helped them move forward.

It is important, though, to remember that their solutions might not fit you exactly, because each person's situation is unique. Still, their insights can give you ideas you can adapt to your own life. Seeing real evidence that others handled fear can give you the push to try it yourself.

---

16. **Knowing When to Seek Professional Help**

Sometimes, fear of the unknown can be very strong and can connect with other worries in your life. If this fear starts to interfere with your everyday tasks, your relationships, or your mental health, it could be time to talk to a counselor or therapist. They can help you uncover deeper causes of fear and teach methods for managing anxiety.

There is no shame in reaching out for help if fear is overwhelming. A mental health professional can offer specific tools, such as cognitive behavioral methods, to guide you through fearful thoughts. Getting help when you need it can prevent fear from growing bigger and interfering with your life plans.

---

17. **Being Kind to Yourself**

Facing the unknown can be stressful, so treat yourself with understanding. You might get frustrated if you do not feel fearless right away, or if you try a new step and it turns out harder than you hoped. Remind yourself that it is normal to have mixed emotions. Encourage yourself the way you would encourage a friend.

Self-kindness can include taking breaks, rewarding yourself for small wins, and speaking gently to yourself when you face tough moments. By being patient and kind, you allow yourself to move at a pace that feels right for you, reducing the pressure that fear often creates.

---

18. **Embracing the Learning Process**

Each time you face the unknown and handle it—whether the outcome is a clear success or not—you learn more about yourself. You discover what your limits are, what interests you, and how you react to stress. Over time, this learning can turn into wisdom that helps you with future unknowns. You might notice patterns: maybe you are always anxious at the start but settle down once you take a small step.

Looking at each new situation as a learning chance can change your attitude toward fear. Instead of seeing the unknown as a threat, see it as a chance to grow in knowledge and life skills. This viewpoint reduces anxiety because learning is something you can benefit from, no matter the outcome.

---

19. **Allowing Time for Adjustment**

When you step into unknown territory, it is normal to feel uneasy for a while. You might need time to settle into a new role, routine, or environment. During this adjustment period, you could feel lonely, unsure, or even second-guess your choice. Recognize that these feelings are part of adapting. Instead of judging yourself for feeling uneasy, see it as a sign that you are doing something unfamiliar, which is how growth often begins.

Give yourself a reasonable period to see how things develop. If it is a new school, maybe give it a semester to see if it gets better. If it is a new job, spend enough time to learn your duties and get to know your team. Often, the worst fear is at the beginning. As you gather experience, the unknown becomes the familiar.

Chapter 4: Using Emotions Wisely

Emotions play a big part in how people make choices. They can guide you toward something that is important or warn you about possible risks. However, emotions can also mislead you if they are too strong or if you do not handle them well. This chapter looks at how to use emotions in a way that helps you rather than confuses you. You will learn about common emotional triggers, how to pause before acting on strong feelings, and ways to turn emotions into useful tools for clearer thinking.

---

1. **How Emotions Influence Decisions**

Emotions are signals that come from deep inside your mind. They can tell you that something feels right or wrong, safe or threatening, exciting or dull. Because these signals arrive so quickly, you might react to them without stopping to think. For example, if you feel angry at a person who cut you off in traffic, you might honk your horn or shout without considering the consequences.

While emotions can be helpful, they are not always accurate. Sometimes, an emotion might be based on a misunderstanding or a small trigger from your past. This is why it is important to notice your emotions but also to check them against facts. By doing so, you can figure out whether your emotional response fits the current situation.

---

2. **Common Emotional Traps**

There are certain emotional states that can push you to make hasty decisions:

- **Overexcitement:** When you are very excited, you might overlook risks or costs. Everything can appear brighter than it is.
- **Anxiety:** Too much worry can make you avoid important steps or miss good opportunities because you only see the potential for harm.
- **Anger:** Anger can push you to act quickly, sometimes causing you to say or do things that damage relationships or lead to outcomes you regret.

- **Sadness or Hopelessness:** Feeling low can make you miss positive details in a situation. You might assume there is no point in trying.

Recognizing these emotional traps can help you slow down and think more carefully when they appear.

---

3. **Pausing Before You React**

One simple but powerful way to manage strong emotions is to pause. When you notice a rush of emotion—be it fear, anger, or excitement—try to take a short break before deciding what to do. This could mean closing your eyes for a few seconds, counting to ten, or taking a few slow breaths. The pause allows your thinking brain to catch up with your emotional brain.

During the pause, name the emotion you are feeling. Say to yourself, "I am feeling angry," or, "I am feeling thrilled." Identifying the emotion can reduce its intensity by helping you see it as a separate thing rather than letting it control you. Once you have named the emotion, ask yourself, "What is the best next step?" This small moment of reflection can lead to choices that are wiser than if you acted on raw feeling alone.

---

4. **Finding Useful Information in Emotions**

Emotions are not the enemy. They can be valuable sources of information. For instance, if you feel uneasy about a plan, that unease might be pointing you toward a real risk you have not addressed. If you feel a spark of excitement about a new idea, that excitement might mean you see potential in it. By exploring the reason behind an emotion, you can find clues that will help you make a better decision.

Try to ask yourself, "Why am I feeling this way?" If you cannot figure it out right away, do not worry. Sometimes the reason is not obvious. But if you keep asking in a calm way, you might find that your emotion is signaling something important. Once you know what that is, you can decide how to deal with it in a reasonable way.

---

5. **Balancing Heart and Mind**

People often talk about using either logic or feeling, as if they are opposites. In fact, the best decisions often come from balancing both. Your logical mind can help you assess facts, numbers, and future outcomes. Your emotional side can show you your values and what you care about most. If you lean too far on logic alone, you might ignore how a choice makes you feel. If you lean too far on emotion, you might ignore important facts.

A balanced approach might look like this: You use logic to list pros and cons. Then you check with your feelings to see which option seems to fit your values and desires. Or you notice a strong emotion first and then use logic to see if that emotion is based on something concrete. This mix gives you a fuller picture.

---

6. **Using Empathy in Decisions**

Empathy is the ability to feel what someone else is feeling. When making choices that affect other people, empathy helps you consider their perspectives. For instance, if you are a team leader at work and you need to assign tasks, you could think about how your decisions might impact team members' workloads and stress. By understanding their feelings, you can make a choice that is fair and caring.

However, too much empathy can be draining if it leads you to neglect your own needs. It is important to balance empathy with practical concerns. You can care about others and still make choices that respect your own time and goals.

---

7. **Avoiding Emotional Contagion**

Emotional contagion is when you catch someone else's emotion as if it were your own. For example, if you are around a group of people who are very anxious about a situation, you might start to feel nervous too, even if you did not feel that way before. This can affect your decisions because you might adopt the crowd's worry instead of making up your own mind.

To avoid emotional contagion, be aware of your own emotional state before you enter a group setting. Notice if your mood suddenly changes after being around certain people. If you find yourself swept up in their emotions, pause and reflect on whether the emotion is actually yours. Sometimes, stepping away from the group for a moment can help you reconnect with your own thoughts.

8. **Managing Anger Constructively**

Anger can be one of the most challenging emotions to handle when making choices. It can make you lash out, speak harsh words, or make snap judgments. Yet anger also can point out that something unfair or wrong is happening. The key is to channel that anger in a way that leads to a helpful outcome rather than harm.

When you feel anger rising, remove yourself from the source if possible. Take a few deep breaths or go for a short walk. Once you are calmer, think about what triggered your anger. Was there an injustice or a boundary crossed? Then focus on how to address that problem in a clear and respectful way. For example, if a coworker's action upset you, you might plan to talk with them privately once you feel ready to speak calmly.

9. **Checking Feelings Against Reality**

Emotions can sometimes distort your view of reality. If you are really sad, you might think nobody cares about you, even though that is not true. If you are overjoyed, you might think a plan is guaranteed to succeed, even though it has risks. One way to stay grounded is to gather facts that confirm or challenge your emotions. If you feel like a failure, look for evidence of times you did well. If you feel unstoppable, list the steps you still need to take.

This is not about dismissing your emotions. It is about ensuring that your decisions benefit from a dose of objectivity. By looking for real-world proof, you can prevent your feelings from pushing you toward extreme views that do not match the situation.

10. Handling Excitement in a Careful Way

Excitement can feel wonderful. It can fuel you to take on big tasks or explore new projects. However, excitement can also blind you to risks or hidden costs. For instance, you might sign up for a challenging program without reading the requirements because you feel so motivated.

To handle excitement wisely, pause to list both the benefits and the possible downsides of the step you want to take. If the excitement still holds up after you look at the facts, it might be a good sign that you are on the right track. If you find yourself ignoring serious concerns, that is a signal to slow down.

---

11. Developing Emotional Awareness

Emotional awareness means being able to notice and name your feelings in real time. This can be challenging at first, but you can practice by checking in with yourself during the day. Ask, "What am I feeling right now?" Even if the answer is "content," "bored," or "irritated," this helps you build a habit of noticing emotions.

Being aware of your emotions does not mean you must act on them immediately. It just means you understand what you are experiencing. This knowledge gives you more control over how you respond. Instead of being pushed around by feelings, you can decide when and how to address them.

---

12. Practicing Calm Discussion

When emotions are running high, it can be hard to have a useful discussion about a decision that involves others. One method to keep things calm is to set ground rules. For example, agree that each person will speak in turns without interruption. Or you might decide to focus on facts first before sharing feelings. These rules help prevent the discussion from becoming a battle of strong emotions.

If someone starts raising their voice or criticizing in a personal way, gently remind them of the ground rules. Suggest taking a short pause to cool off if needed. Calm discussion does not mean ignoring feelings; it means giving them a space where they can be heard without taking over the whole conversation.

13. Learning to Let Go of Negative Feelings

Sometimes you might hold onto feelings like resentment or jealousy for a long time. These feelings can cloud your judgment and push you toward decisions that are not in your best interest. For example, you might refuse a good offer just because you are angry at the person who made it, even though taking the offer would help you.

Letting go does not mean pretending the hurt never happened. It means choosing not to keep feeding that emotion. You can do this by focusing on the present and the future rather than replaying past issues. If the feeling is strong, talking to a counselor or a trusted friend might help you process it.

---

14. Knowing Your Emotional Triggers

Everyone has emotional triggers—topics or situations that spark a strong reaction. Yours might be related to feeling disrespected, losing control, or remembering a painful event. By identifying these triggers ahead of time, you can prepare yourself before you face them. For instance, if you know that last-minute changes upset you, you can plan how to respond calmly if they occur.

Part of handling triggers is understanding why they affect you so much. Maybe you felt ignored as a child, and now you feel anger if you think you are being ignored at work. Recognizing the root can help you see the present moment more clearly and not let old wounds control new decisions.

---

15. Helping Others with Their Emotions

Sometimes, the best way to keep your own emotions steady is to help someone else calm down. If you are in a group setting and someone is upset, you can offer a listening ear or a kind word. By reducing their emotional intensity, you reduce the chance of a heated environment that could pull you in. This does not mean you have to fix everything for them, but simply being supportive can help everyone return to a clearer mindset.

Keep in mind that helping others should not come at the cost of ignoring your own emotional needs. Make sure you feel stable enough to be supportive. If you are also upset, it might be best to step away and calm yourself before offering help.

16. Turning Emotional Energy into Action

Emotions carry energy. If you feel passionate about an issue, that passion can give you the drive to make a difference. If you feel anger about an unfair situation, that anger can push you to stand up for what is right. The trick is to guide that energy productively rather than letting it burn out of control.

Ask yourself, "What can I do about this feeling?" If it is a positive feeling like hope, you might use it to set goals. If it is a negative feeling like anger, you might channel it into writing a letter, organizing a complaint, or seeking an answer to the problem. By focusing the energy on a clear action, you turn raw feeling into progress.

17. Building Emotional Resilience

Emotional resilience is the ability to bounce back from setbacks or stressful events. When you are resilient, you can face tough emotions without being trapped by them. You learn from difficulties and keep going. To build resilience, practice healthy habits like good sleep, exercise, and supportive friendships. These basics help keep your mood more steady.

You can also practice coping skills, such as deep breathing or light physical activity, when you feel overwhelmed. Over time, these habits strengthen your ability to handle emotional storms. Resilience does not mean you never feel strong emotions; it means you know how to come back to a calm place after you do.

18. Avoiding Quick Fixes for Emotional Pain

Sometimes people look for quick fixes, like buying something expensive to feel better or eating unhealthy foods to cope with sadness. While these might bring short relief, they do not solve the real problem. In fact, they can create new issues, such as money trouble or health problems.

Instead of seeking a quick fix, try to understand what the emotion is telling you. If you are sad, maybe it is because you feel lonely, and what you really need is to reach out to a friend. If you are stressed, perhaps you need rest or to reduce your workload. By looking for the root cause of the emotion, you can choose a solution that truly helps.

---

19. Keeping Track of Emotional Patterns

A helpful exercise is to keep a short journal of your feelings and the decisions you make when you have them. Over a few weeks, you might notice certain patterns. Maybe you see that every time you feel anxious in the evening, you decide to skip your reading or study time. Or perhaps you see that after a short exercise routine, you feel more motivated to follow through on a plan.

By spotting these patterns, you can make changes. If you always skip important tasks because of evening anxiety, you could try doing those tasks earlier in the day or learning a relaxation method. Tracking your emotions and actions shows you how they connect, which helps you use your feelings more wisely.

---

20. Moving Forward with Emotional Wisdom

Using emotions wisely means accepting them as part of who you are without letting them run the show. You can learn to pause before reacting, to check facts, and to take care of your emotional health so you can make calmer, clearer decisions. It is a skill that grows with time and practice.

As you become more aware of your emotions, you will find that decision-making becomes less stressful. You will see that emotions are signals to help you pay attention to what matters, but they do not have to be your only guide. Whether you are feeling excited about a new plan or worried about a potential risk, you can combine that feeling with logic and self-awareness. In doing so, you create a firm foundation for decisions that match your real needs and values.

Emotions are a powerful part of being human. They can enrich your life when understood and used well. By treating them as helpers rather than uninvited guests, you take a strong step toward making good choices that reflect both your heart and your mind.

Chapter 5: Building Self-Confidence

Self-confidence is the belief that you can handle what life brings your way. It is not about thinking you are perfect or better than others. It is about trusting your ability to learn, adapt, and push through barriers. This chapter explains why self-confidence matters, how it shapes your decisions, and methods to strengthen it. By the end, you will see that building self-confidence is an ongoing process that anyone can work on, no matter their starting point.

---

1. **Why Self-Confidence Matters**

When you have confidence in yourself, you are more likely to try new things and stick with them when they get tough. This makes it easier to grow your skills or explore new areas. People with healthy self-confidence do not fear mistakes as much, because they believe they can recover and learn from any slip-ups. A person who trusts themselves is also more willing to speak up, offer ideas, and stand by choices that match their personal values.

Low self-confidence, however, can make you hesitant. You might avoid taking reasonable risks or speaking your mind. You might feel insecure when you compare yourself to others, which can leave you doubting even your positive traits. Decisions become harder because you fear making the "wrong" move or being judged. Building self-confidence helps you face these worries with a stronger attitude.

---

2. **Knowing the Difference Between Healthy and False Confidence**

Confidence should not be confused with arrogance. Arrogance happens when someone believes they are always right or better than everyone else. This attitude often hides a shaky sense of self-worth. True confidence, by contrast, is balanced. You acknowledge you have strong points and areas where you need to improve. You feel good about what you can do, but you do not look down on others.

False confidence can also appear when a person relies too much on praise from other people. If they do not get that outside approval, their sense of self-worth collapses. Real confidence comes from within. It might be boosted when others notice your efforts, but it does not rely on that praise as its main source of strength.

---

3. **Looking at Past Achievements**

A good first step in building self-confidence is to look at what you have already done well. These can be small wins or bigger accomplishments. Perhaps you learned a new skill, helped someone through a tough time, or overcame a personal fear. Make a list of these wins, even if they seem minor. Often, people forget the things they have managed to do over the years.

When you read this list, you can see proof that you can succeed. You have done it before in other areas, so why not now in a new challenge? If you like, keep this list somewhere you can see it daily. It is a reminder that you are capable, even when you feel uncertain. Recalling past achievements does not mean you stop trying to grow; it just gives you a base of evidence that you can build upon.

---

4. **Acknowledging Your Strengths**

Everyone has unique strengths. Some people are good at organizing projects. Others are creative in how they solve problems. Some are patient listeners, while others are great at making plans. By spotting your strengths, you can direct your time toward what you are naturally good at. This does not mean you ignore weaker areas. Rather, it means you use your main strengths as a starting point for confidence.

Try to identify at least three strengths you have. If you struggle to see them, ask people who know you well. They might say you are calm under pressure, kind when helping friends, or focused on tasks. After you collect these responses, reflect on how you can use these traits more often. For instance, if you are very organized, you might take the lead in planning group events.

---

5. **Setting Realistic Goals**

One major cause of low self-confidence is setting goals that are too big or too vague. For example, if you decide you want to master a complicated subject in a few days, you may feel discouraged when you cannot do it so quickly. Instead, break large goals into smaller steps. By doing this, you give yourself clear tasks that you can finish within a short time.

Each completed step becomes another reason to believe in yourself. Instead of only looking at a big end target—like learning a foreign language—focus on hitting small daily or weekly milestones, such as memorizing a list of words or practicing speaking for 15 minutes a day. With each step finished, your self-confidence grows because you see real proof that you can make progress.

---

6. **Learning from Errors**

Mistakes and errors happen to everyone, even the most confident people. What makes a difference is how you react. If you treat mistakes as proof that you are a failure, your self-confidence will drop. But if you view mistakes as a normal part of trying something new, you can recover faster and come away with new lessons.

Consider an error as a signal that something needs adjustment. Maybe you need to practice more, do better research, or manage your time differently. Each correction makes you stronger for your next attempt. By seeing mistakes in this practical, helpful way, you remove the personal blame and focus on growth instead. Over time, you build the courage to face bigger challenges because you know a mistake is not the end of your efforts.

---

7. **Changing Negative Self-Talk**

Negative self-talk is the habit of putting yourself down in your own thoughts. You might say, "I am just not good at anything" or "I will mess this up." These statements erode confidence over time and make you less likely to try. To turn this around, first notice when negative thoughts arise. Then, replace them with more balanced thoughts.

Instead of, "I am terrible at this," try, "I need more practice to get better." Instead of, "I always fail," say, "Sometimes I succeed, and sometimes I have to learn from what did not work." This shift takes effort, but it helps you see that your abilities are not fixed. They can grow with time and practice. Gradually, your inner voice becomes more supportive.

8. **Surrounding Yourself with Encouraging People**

The people around you can have a big impact on how you view yourself. If you spend time with those who constantly criticize or doubt you, it can lower your self-confidence. On the other hand, supportive friends, family, or mentors can help you believe in yourself. They cheer you on, give constructive feedback, and celebrate your efforts rather than just the outcome.

Look for groups, clubs, or social circles where people share a positive mindset. Being in a hopeful and uplifting environment makes it easier to risk new things. You do not need to abandon your current friends, but try to balance your social life so you have enough sources of positivity. Over time, this can reshape your overall attitude.

9. **Practicing Confident Body Language**

Body language can send signals to your mind about how you feel. Standing tall, making eye contact, and speaking in a clear voice can actually boost your inner sense of confidence. This does not mean you should pretend to be someone you are not. Rather, it is about aligning your outside posture with the healthy confidence you are building inside.

Try small changes like walking with your head up and shoulders back. Notice how you feel when you do so. If you catch yourself slouching or avoiding eye contact, correct it gently. Over time, this practice becomes a habit. It is a simple trick, but it can have a surprising effect on both how you see yourself and how others see you.

10. Taking Calculated Risks

You build more self-confidence when you see yourself handling challenges successfully. That means saying yes to some risks, but doing so in a smart way. A calculated risk is one where you weigh the possible downsides and likely upsides, then decide that trying is worth it. For instance, you might take on a slightly bigger project at work than you usually do. You check how much time it will take and whether you have the skills, and then you plan accordingly.

When you succeed, you expand your idea of what you can do. Even if you do not get the perfect result, you learn valuable lessons. Each try helps you see that you can handle more than you once thought. Over time, your comfort zone expands, and so does your confidence.

---

11. Avoiding Constant Comparisons

Comparing yourself to others can hurt your self-confidence if you focus on their achievements and ignore your own. There will always be someone who does something better than you. That does not mean you are unworthy or a failure. Instead of comparing, look at your own progress. Are you doing better than you did last month or last year?

If you must compare, do it in a way that lifts you up rather than puts you down. You might notice how a skilled person does something and learn from it. Use it as inspiration, not as a reason to feel smaller. Remember, each person has a different set of strengths, interests, and life paths. Your path is yours alone, and it does not have to match anyone else's timeline.

---

12. Building Skills Step by Step

Confidence often comes from knowing you have real ability in something. Building a skill is a sure way to strengthen that confidence. For example, if you want to become a better public speaker, you might start by giving short talks in front of a small group. Later, you move to larger audiences. Each time you improve a bit, your belief in your speaking ability grows.

Follow a process: set a skill goal, plan practice sessions, and track your improvements. This methodical approach shows you clear evidence of progress. Even if you have never tried something before, you can develop a sense of confidence by focusing on slow and steady skill-building rather than jumping in blindly.

---

13. Handling Criticism in a Healthy Way

Criticism can hurt if you are not used to it, but it can also point out areas where you can improve. When someone criticizes you, try to see if they have a point. Is there something useful you can take from their words? If yes, take that part and use it to grow. If the criticism is just mean or not based on facts, remind yourself that not all opinions are valid.

Learning to handle criticism helps you stay focused on your path rather than letting negative remarks knock you down. You can decide which feedback to keep and which to throw away. This sense of control over external opinions is a key part of self-confidence, because it shows you that you, not others, have the final say in who you are.

---

14. Creating Daily Routines That Boost Confidence

A morning routine or an evening routine can set the tone for how you feel about yourself. For instance, you might start the day by reviewing your schedule, saying a quick statement of encouragement to yourself, or writing down a small goal for the day. At night, you could reflect on one thing you did well. These simple practices remind you to see your own strengths and progress regularly.

Another helpful routine is mindful breathing or gentle exercise. Taking a few minutes to clear your mind and connect with your body can reduce stress and keep you balanced. This sense of calm can make it easier to maintain a steady level of self-confidence, instead of having it go up and down with daily events.

---

15. **Using Visualization**

Visualization means creating a clear mental picture of yourself doing something successfully. Athletes often use this method to see themselves performing well before a competition. You can do the same for any task or goal. Before a test, picture yourself answering questions calmly. Before a new challenge at work, see yourself handling it with skill.

By visualizing success, you prime your brain for the real thing. This does not guarantee everything will go perfectly, but it does help you feel more prepared. Confidence grows when your mind is used to the idea that you can perform the task well. You are less likely to walk into the situation with negative images that lower your courage.

---

16. **Embracing Imperfection**

No one is perfect, and trying to be can hurt your self-confidence because you set standards that are impossible to meet. Embracing imperfection means you accept that flaws or mistakes are part of being human. You still work hard, but you do not tie your sense of worth to a flawless performance.

When you make a slip, remind yourself it is normal. Focus on what you can learn instead of beating yourself up. This mindset helps you bounce back quickly and preserves your self-confidence. By accepting that some level of imperfection is inevitable, you free yourself from the burden of trying to appear flawless to yourself or others.

---

17. **Giving Yourself Credit for Small Wins**

You do not have to wait for a massive victory to feel good about what you have done. Small wins, like finishing a task on time or remembering to practice a new skill, matter too. Acknowledging these small steps can give you steady boosts of self-confidence. It shifts your focus from what you have not done to what you have accomplished.

Try keeping a simple record of wins each day. They can be as minor as replying to an important message or organizing a messy space. By noting them, you train your mind to look for progress rather than shortfalls. Over time, these bits of positive evidence build a solid foundation for your confidence.

18. Standing Up for Your Own Needs

Confidence also means you feel able to speak up when something is not working for you. This might be at school, at work, or in personal relationships. If you constantly remain silent about your needs, you may start feeling powerless or undervalued. The act of politely and firmly stating what you need can remind you that you have a voice and that it matters.

This does not mean ignoring other people's needs. It just means you place your needs on the table alongside theirs. Whether it is asking for help, discussing a problem, or saying no to a request, standing up for yourself in a calm way boosts self-esteem. You show yourself that you respect your own well-being enough to speak out.

19. Staying True to Your Values

Your values are what you believe is right and important. Confidence grows when your actions match those values. If kindness is a key value for you, showing kindness in your daily actions can make you feel good about who you are. If you value honesty, being truthful in tough situations can make you feel proud.

On the other hand, going against your core values can drain confidence, because deep down you know you are not acting in line with who you want to be. Keeping your values close and acting in ways that fit them builds inner harmony. This harmony feeds self-confidence because you trust yourself to do what you believe is right.

20. Maintaining Progress Over Time

Building self-confidence is not a one-time event; it is an ongoing process. There will be ups and downs. You might feel very sure of yourself one week and then face a setback that shakes you the next. The important thing is to keep going. If you find your confidence slipping, revisit the methods that helped you before:

- Review your list of achievements.
- Remind yourself of your main strengths.
- Tweak your goals to make them more manageable.
- Practice more positive self-talk.

With consistent effort, you will notice that each time you bounce back a bit faster. Over months and years, your self-confidence can become a stable part of who you are, rather than something that comes and goes based on outside opinions or recent events.

Final Thoughts on Building Self-Confidence

Self-confidence opens doors to new opportunities, richer relationships, and a better sense of self. It is not about bragging; it is about recognizing that you have the skills and mindset to figure things out, even when they are tough. By applying the strategies in this chapter—setting realistic goals, learning from errors, using positive self-talk, and more—you can slowly raise your self-confidence. It will not happen overnight, but each small step gives you more proof that you can trust yourself. With time and practice, you build a solid inner belief that helps you face life's options with strength and clear thinking.

Chapter 6: Coping with Outside Pressures

Making decisions can be hard when many voices from the world around you weigh in. These outside pressures might come from your family, friends, social media, or the wider culture. At times, their opinions and demands can clash with what you want for yourself. You might feel torn between fitting in and following your own path. This chapter explores ways to handle outside pressures so you can choose with a clear mind.

---

1. **Understanding External Influences**

External influences affect your thinking more than you might realize. They can shape your goals and even your sense of self. For example, family members might have set ideas about your future career. Friends could urge you to follow a certain fashion trend or join in certain activities. Ads and social media posts show you what "successful" people look like, pressuring you to measure up.

Sometimes, these influences can be good. Advice from a parent or an older sibling might help you avoid mistakes. Observing a successful person in your field can give you practical tips to improve. The problem arises when these pressures push you to do things that do not suit your own values, skills, or life situation. That is when you need to pause and think about what truly feels right.

---

2. **Spotting Harmful Pressures**

Not all outside pressure is harmful, so it is important to tell the difference between helpful guidance and unwanted control. Harmful pressure may include:

- **Excessive Comparisons**: People keep pointing out how you should be like someone else.
- **Emotional Manipulation**: Guilt-trips or threats if you do not do what they say.
- **Rigid Rules**: Commands that leave no room for discussion.
- **Peer Pressure**: Friends pushing you to do something that goes against your values.

When you notice these signs, it is a signal to protect your independence. You can still respect the people offering advice, but you do not have to give in to their pressure if it harms your well-being.

---

3. Sorting Helpful Advice from Noise

Sometimes, outside opinions are given as well-meaning advice. Your teacher might suggest a certain path, or your neighbor might offer tips. Sorting helpful advice from noise involves asking:

1. **Does this advice align with my values and goals?** If it supports what you care about, it might be worth considering.
2. **Is the person giving the advice knowledgeable about the topic?** If they have real experience, their advice may hold weight.
3. **Are they considering my situation?** If they are just pushing their own viewpoint without looking at your needs, you can take the advice with caution.

By asking these questions, you can filter out what does not serve you. You do not need to be rude, but you can politely decide which advice to keep.

---

4. Balancing Family Expectations

Family can have a powerful role in shaping your decisions, especially if you live with them. Parents or relatives might want you to follow a path they believe is best. This often comes from a place of caring, but it can create stress if your own dreams differ from theirs.

A good approach is to have calm talks with family members. Explain your perspective and the reasons behind your choice. Show them that you are thinking carefully rather than acting on a whim. You might find that once they see your plan, they are more supportive. If they still disagree, try to maintain a respectful stance. Let them know you value their concern but also need space to make your own decisions. Balancing your wishes with family input is tricky, but it can be done with openness and patience.

5. **Dealing with Friends' Opinions**

Friends can influence you because you want to stay on good terms with them. You might worry that if you go against their wishes, you will be left out. In some cases, this is a normal part of friendship—friends suggest ideas, and you work together. But if you feel you are always giving in or doing things that make you uncomfortable, it is time to step back and reflect.

Communication is key. Speak honestly with your friends. You might say, "I understand why you want to do this, but it does not feel right for me." Genuine friends will hear you out, even if they do not agree. If a friend pressures you in ways that make you uneasy, ask yourself if that friendship is as supportive as it should be. True friends respect personal limits.

---

6. **Handling Cultural and Social Pressures**

Culture sets standards of what is considered normal or acceptable, and these standards vary widely. In some places, people are pushed to marry young; in others, they are pushed to focus on a career first. Social media can also shape cultural pressure by showing you an endless stream of "perfect" lives, suggesting you should match that image.

When facing these broad pressures, remind yourself that cultural norms are not one-size-fits-all. You can embrace parts of your culture that feel meaningful and valuable, yet still make personal choices where you disagree. For instance, you might follow some traditions that reflect your heritage, but politely decline others that do not match your beliefs. Culture can enrich your life, but it should not force you into decisions that go against who you are.

---

7. **Navigating Social Media Influence**

Social media can intensify outside pressure. You see posts of people traveling, landing impressive jobs, or showing off material possessions, which might make you feel you should do the same. This pressure is often based on an edited version of reality. People tend to share their best moments, not their daily struggles.

A way to cope is to set healthy boundaries on social media. Limit how much time you spend scrolling, and remember that each post is just a glimpse. Notice when you start feeling envy or pressure to be like someone else. Ask yourself if you genuinely want that lifestyle or if you just think you should want it because it looks appealing on a screen. Stepping away from constant comparison can free you to make decisions based on your own real interests.

---

8. **Practicing Assertive Communication**

Assertive communication means stating your needs and feelings in a way that respects both you and the other person. It is different from being passive (where you say nothing) and different from being aggressive (where you try to force your view). When people try to sway you, an assertive response might be, "I hear what you are saying, but I see things differently," or, "Thank you for your suggestion, but I need some time to think about it."

This firm yet respectful style can disarm pushy people. It also reminds you that you have a right to your own thoughts and decisions. If they keep pushing, you can repeat the same statement. Over time, they may learn that you stand by your choices.

---

9. **Setting Personal Boundaries**

Boundaries are lines that define what you feel is acceptable and what is not. They protect your time, your emotions, and your values. For instance, you can set a boundary that says you will not discuss certain personal topics with casual acquaintances. You might decide you will only check social media once a day to limit outside influence. Or you might refuse to engage in certain conversations that always end up in negative arguments.

Clearly stating your boundaries can feel awkward at first, but it gets easier with practice. Boundaries teach others how to interact with you. They also remind you that your comfort matters. Whether with family, friends, or in a workplace, healthy boundaries prevent people from steering your life in ways you do not want.

10. **Finding Safe Spaces for Self-Expression**

Sometimes, outside pressures feel overwhelming because you do not have a place to express your true thoughts. Finding a safe space—like a trusted friend, a support group, or an online forum—can help you work through confusion. In these spaces, you can share ideas without fear of judgment. You might discover that other people face the same outside pressures you do, which can make you feel less alone.

In a safe space, you can practice explaining your views. You can get feedback from people who understand or respect you. This practice can build up your confidence to handle tougher conversations in the broader world. You are free to explore different angles without worrying that someone will force their opinions on you.

---

11. **Time Management as Protection**

Outside pressures can also involve people pushing you to do more than you can handle. For instance, your boss might want you to stay late, your friends might want you to go out every weekend, and your family might want you to visit often. Each request might be fine on its own, but together they overload your schedule.

Learn to protect your time by planning in advance. Look at your calendar and see how much space you actually have for extra tasks or social events. If you are already at capacity, politely say no or suggest another time. This is not selfish; it is a practical way to ensure that other people's agendas do not consume your whole life. By managing your time well, you guard your mental and emotional energy.

---

12. **Avoiding the Trap of Trying to Please Everyone**

Trying to please everyone usually ends up pleasing no one, especially yourself. You might say yes to too many requests, take on too many responsibilities, or keep your real opinions hidden. Over time, this can lead to stress and a loss of your personal identity.

Instead, pick a few things that really matter to you or that you can do well for others. Say yes to those, and politely decline the rest. This approach allows you to maintain good relationships without being pulled in every direction. It also helps others see that you have limits. They may not always like it, but they will learn that you are making balanced, thoughtful choices, not just acting out of a need for approval.

---

13. Taking a Step Back to Reflect

When you feel buried under outside pressure, take a pause. You can do this by finding a quiet spot and taking a few slow breaths. Then ask yourself:

- "What do I really want out of this situation?"
- "Are these pressures helping me get there, or distracting me?"
- "What steps can I take that match my own values?"

This reflection can clear your mind of the noise. It allows you to act from a place of clarity instead of reacting to whatever push or pull comes your way. Even a five-minute break can make a big difference in regaining control over your decisions.

---

14. Learning to Say "No" Politely

Saying no can feel uncomfortable, especially if you worry about disappointing someone. However, "no" is a powerful word that can protect you from unwanted tasks, draining social events, or questionable requests. There are ways to say no that are respectful and not rude. For example:

- "I appreciate the offer, but I have other priorities right now."
- "I understand why this matters to you, but I am unable to help at this time."
- "I need to focus on my current project, so I cannot commit to another activity."

By offering a clear reason—without over-explaining—you show that your no is not personal, but based on your own limits or plans. This honesty can actually build respect in the long run.

15. Recognizing Manipulative Tactics

In some cases, people might use manipulative tactics to get you to do what they want. These can include:

- **Guilt Tripping**: "If you cared about me, you would do this."
- **Shaming**: "Only a bad friend would say no."
- **Withholding Approval**: "I will think less of you if you do not agree."

When you sense manipulation, remind yourself that real respect does not involve playing such games. Stay calm and repeat your stance. You might say, "I am sorry if you feel hurt, but I have to make a choice that is right for me." It can be hard to stand firm, but giving in to manipulation often leads to regret.

---

16. Seeking Help When Pressures Are Overwhelming

If outside pressures are causing severe stress, anxiety, or sadness, consider talking to a counselor or a trusted professional. They can help you see patterns in the types of pressure you face and develop personalized ways to cope. There is no shame in reaching out for help, especially if you feel trapped.

Support groups can also be beneficial. For example, if your family is pressuring you about a life choice, talking to others who have faced similar family dynamics can bring insight. Hearing different stories might give you ideas for how to handle your situation. The key is not to stay isolated in your struggle.

---

17. Reminding Yourself of Personal Goals

One of the best defenses against outside pressure is having clear personal goals. When you know what you want, it becomes easier to see if a suggestion or demand fits that aim or not. Write down your top three goals for the next six months or year. Keep them in a place you check often, such as on your phone or a small notebook.

When someone pushes you to do something, compare it to your goals. Ask: "Does this action bring me closer to or further from where I want to be?" If it aligns, then maybe you can say yes. If not, a polite no might be better for your long-term path. Having this reference point can keep you from drifting under everyone else's agendas.

18. Focusing on Your Inner Values

While goals often change over time, core values tend to be more stable. They are the guiding principles about how you want to live. Maybe you value honesty, caring for others, or personal growth. Keeping these values in mind helps you see through outside pressures that conflict with your moral code.

For instance, if a situation asks you to be dishonest or hurt someone else to get ahead, you can firmly refuse because it clashes with your sense of right and wrong. Standing by your values might be uncomfortable in the short term, but it builds inner respect and a sense of integrity that no outside force can shake.

19. Developing Emotional Independence

Emotional independence means you do not rely completely on others for how you feel about yourself. Of course, we all want connection, love, and approval, but it can become a problem if your entire self-worth depends on what others think. By building self-confidence (as discussed in the previous chapter) and knowing your own values, you create an inner compass. This helps you stay steady even if someone criticizes or tries to steer you in an unwanted direction.

You can practice emotional independence by noticing when you feel upset or worried just because someone disapproved of you. Ask yourself: "Is their view more important than my own informed decision?" or "Could they be projecting their own issues onto me?" This approach helps you see that outside judgments are not always a fair measure of your worth.

20. Making Decisions That Reflect Your True Self

In the end, coping with outside pressures is about learning to make decisions that match who you really are and what you genuinely want. That does not mean ignoring all advice or being stubborn. It means being open to good input, while remembering that you have the final say.

- **Listen to opinions, but do not let them drown out your own voice.**
- **Stay respectful, but protect your right to decide for yourself.**
- **Stay true to your goals and values, even if it upsets some people.**

Over time, you will notice that the more you choose in line with your real self, the calmer and clearer you feel. Outside pressures become easier to navigate because you no longer need constant approval or fear others' disapproval. Your life starts to feel like it belongs to you, rather than to everyone else.

Closing Thoughts on Coping with Outside Pressures

Outside pressures can be loud and persistent, but they do not have to control you. By setting boundaries, speaking assertively, sorting helpful advice from harmful demands, and holding tight to your own goals and values, you can keep a strong sense of self. Though it can be uncomfortable at times, this approach leads to decisions that you can stand by, confident that they fit the person you want to be. When you can manage outside pressures, you take one more step toward making clear, steady choices that truly serve you.

Chapter 7: Thinking About Possible Outcomes

When you are facing a choice, it helps to think ahead about what could happen. Instead of making a quick guess, you can map out the possible results. This can prevent you from being caught off guard later. This chapter is all about looking at different paths the future might take, comparing them, and picking the path that fits your aims. You will learn simple methods to plan for results, weigh pros and cons, and decide if a risk is worth it.

---

1. **Why It Helps to Look Ahead**

People often make choices based on how they feel in the moment. While feelings matter, you also want to see where that choice may lead. For example, if you are picking between two jobs, it is wise to think not only about salary or location right now, but also about how each job could shape your skills, future opportunities, and daily life. By looking ahead, you paint a clearer picture that goes beyond short-term satisfaction.

This skill can also spare you trouble. Let's say a friend invites you to join a new sports club. You might think, "Sure, sounds good." But if you look ahead, you might see that it conflicts with your study schedule. Or, you might realize that the cost of the club plus gear is more than you can handle. Thinking ahead gives you a preview of possible roadblocks. Of course, you cannot predict everything, but even a rough sketch of the future is better than none.

---

2. **Imagining Different Scenarios**

A simple way to look at possible outcomes is to imagine different "what if" scenarios. For example:

- **Best Case:** Everything goes smoothly, no big problems arise, and you get a great result.
- **Likely Case:** Some things go well, some problems pop up, and you end up with a result that is in-between.
- **Worst Case:** Many problems happen, and you face a difficult or unpleasant result.

By writing down these three scenarios, you start to see the range of what might happen. You can then ask yourself how you would respond in each situation. For the worst case, you can plan ways to deal with it. For the best case, you can note how to make the most of it. This process can calm nerves because it makes uncertainty feel more manageable and less mysterious.

---

3. **Using Basic Pros and Cons**

The pros and cons list is one of the simplest tools for weighing outcomes. You split a page into two columns: pros on one side, cons on the other. Then you list all the good points and all the negative points for each choice you have. This does not decide for you automatically, but it helps you see everything in front of you.

Sometimes, the number of pros and cons is not enough by itself, because certain points matter more than others. For instance, you might have ten small pros and one very large con that outweighs them. In this case, you can rate each item by importance. For instance, on a scale of 1 to 5, how big is this pro or con? Then add up the totals. If one choice has a much higher total of pros than cons, it might be the better path.

---

4. **Weighing Short-Term vs. Long-Term**

A common issue in decision-making is deciding whether to focus on short-term or long-term benefits. Some choices bring a quick reward now, but might limit your future. Other choices might be hard at first but could open bigger doors later. For example, paying for a course might be costly in the short run, but learning the skills could lead to better job options. Spending your savings on a short vacation might be fun now, but then you do not have that money for other goals.

When you think about possible outcomes, divide them into short-term and long-term categories. Short-term covers the next few days or weeks, while long-term might look at months, years, or even longer. Think about what matters most to you. Do you want immediate enjoyment, or would you rather invest in a result that takes time to grow? Sometimes a balance is possible, but if not, it helps to be clear which side you are choosing and why.

5. Making a Decision Tree

A decision tree is a simple diagram showing how each choice might unfold into new results or new choices. You start with your main question at the top (e.g., "Should I move to a new city?"). Then you draw branches for each possible answer ("Yes" or "No"). From each branch, you add more branches for the outcomes that could happen under that decision.

For example, if you say "Yes" to moving, the next set of branches might be about finding a place to live, picking a job, or adjusting to a new community. If you say "No," the branches might be about staying where you are, improving your current home, or seeking a different path to grow. Seeing your choices in a tree form can uncover hidden routes you had not noticed. It can also show you that many small choices come after the big one, so you do not have to have everything figured out at once.

---

6. Considering Probability

Some outcomes are more likely than others. If you are thinking of starting a small business, there might be a 50% chance you break even, a 20% chance you make a large profit, and a 30% chance you take a loss. These are rough guesses, of course, but assigning likelihoods can help you compare the expected result of each path.

If the chance of success is very low, you might decide it is not worth the time and money. If the chance is high, you might feel more confident. Even if the chance is moderate, you might still proceed if the reward for success is big enough and if you can handle the risk of failure. Just remember that no matter how carefully you guess, reality can still go another way. Probability is a guide, not a guarantee.

---

7. Checking for Hidden Costs or Benefits

Sometimes a choice has hidden costs or benefits that are not obvious at first. For example, suppose you are offered a higher-paying job, but it requires a longer commute. The extra money might look great on paper, but you also need to consider the price of gas or train fare, plus the extra hours you spend traveling. On the other hand, you might join a community club that does not pay you anything, but you gain valuable skills and friendships that could lead to paid opportunities later. Those are hidden benefits.

Try to look beyond the surface. Ask yourself what resources—like time, money, energy, or stress management—each choice might use up. Also ask what unexpected advantages might come from it, such as meeting new people, learning new skills, or improving your health. By spotting these hidden angles, you get a fuller picture of the outcomes.

---

8. **Breaking Big Choices into Smaller Steps**

Often, a big choice looks scary because you see a lot of unknowns at once. You can make this easier by breaking it into smaller steps. Instead of deciding all at once whether you will move to another country, start by choosing to research housing, job options, or visa requirements. Then decide which region appeals to you most. Step by step, you gather facts that help you see the possible outcomes more clearly.

Each step is a mini-choice with its own outcomes. For instance, if your research shows the cost of living is too high in one area, you can switch your focus to a different area. If you see there are more job openings than you thought, you may feel more optimistic. By the time you make the final decision, you have already tested several small outcomes that guide you.

---

9. **Being Realistic About Best and Worst Outcomes**

Earlier in this chapter, we talked about the best-case and worst-case scenarios. It is important to be realistic about them. It is easy to dream of the best outcome and forget that it might need extra work or luck. Likewise, it is easy to dread the worst outcome and assume it will happen no matter what. A realistic view recognizes that good results usually involve some effort and planning, and that the worst outcomes are sometimes avoidable or fixable.

Think about ways to make the best outcome more likely. Could you gather extra knowledge, ask for help from an expert, or give yourself more time to prepare? Also, think about ways to prevent or handle the worst outcome. Could you buy insurance, set aside savings, or have a backup plan? This mindset keeps your view balanced and helps you feel more prepared.

---

10. Connecting Outcomes to Your Personal Values

In a previous chapter, we discussed how values guide what you find important. When you think about outcomes, see if they match your values. For instance, if you value family closeness, and one choice leads to living far away from relatives, that might create conflict in your mind. If you value creativity, but a certain path offers no room for creative thinking, you might feel unhappy later.

If you notice a mismatch between an outcome and your values, think about ways to adjust. Maybe you can choose a path that still aligns with your goals but keeps you close to family. Or maybe you can add a side project that lets you be creative even if your main job is not. Seeing how each outcome fits (or does not fit) your values can be a deciding factor.

---

11. Planning for the Ripple Effect

Your choice might cause a ripple effect in other areas of life. For example, picking a new hobby could shift how much time you have for your friends or how you spend your weekends. Choosing to invest money in a project could affect your travel plans or your ability to handle emergencies. These ripples can be positive if they lead to improvement or learning, or they can be negative if they create more stress.

When you plan for outcomes, ask yourself who or what else might be affected by your decision. Could it cause conflict with a coworker, or maybe strengthen a bond with a neighbor? Could it make you busier on weekdays or freer on weekends? By checking for ripples, you reduce the risk of unpleasant surprises and can prepare for side effects that come with the main outcome.

12. Talking Through Outcomes with Others

Discussing possible outcomes with trusted people can bring new ideas you did not think of on your own. They might have been in a similar situation and can tell you how it turned out for them. They might spot a hidden benefit or risk that you missed. Keep in mind that their experience might be different from yours, but hearing different perspectives is still valuable.

Try to pick people who will be honest and supportive, rather than those who might push you to do what they want. A balanced friend or mentor can ask good questions like, "What do you think might happen if…?" or "Have you thought about how this will affect…?" This can help you broaden your view of the possible outcomes.

---

13. Using Time to Your Advantage

If you have enough time before making a choice, use it wisely. Some people rush to decide without looking into details. Others waste time by putting off the decision and letting stress build. The best approach is to give yourself a set period to gather information and evaluate possible outcomes, then pick a date when you will decide.

During that set period, avoid last-minute cramming. Spread out your research or thinking sessions. Let your mind process ideas slowly so you can think of new angles. If you feel stuck, step away for a bit and then come back. Your brain often works in the background, making connections that help you see outcomes more clearly when you return to the question.

---

14. Caution with Overthinking

While mapping outcomes is good, beware of overthinking. If you try to account for every tiny possibility, you might never decide. Perfect information is hard to get, and life always includes a bit of risk. At some point, you have to trust the facts and feelings you have gathered and make a move.

A sign that you might be overthinking is when you keep re-reading the same facts or re-listing the same pros and cons without any new insight. You might feel stuck in a loop. If that happens, ask yourself if you have enough key information to decide. If the answer is yes, it might be time to act and see how it goes.

---

15. Adapting as New Facts Appear

Even after you pick a path, outcomes can shift if new information arises. Maybe a choice that looked good at first becomes less appealing because the conditions changed. In that case, do not be afraid to pivot if it is still possible. For example, if you discover that a certain company is no longer hiring, you might turn your attention to a similar company or a different field.

This does not mean switching choices whenever you feel uncertain. You do not want to be inconsistent. However, if a major piece of news changes the landscape, it is wise to reevaluate. Your original plan was based on the facts you had at the time. If the facts shift, your plan might need a small update or a complete change.

---

16. Balancing Gut Feelings and Logic

Sometimes your gut feeling points you in a certain direction, and sometimes your logical analysis points somewhere else. How do you handle this conflict? One way is to look at whether your gut feeling might be warning you of something logical that you have not noticed yet. Are you missing a crucial fact or ignoring a risk?

On the other hand, your gut might reflect your personal values or hopes, which are also important. If your logical approach leads you to a path that feels entirely wrong in your heart, you may be ignoring what truly matters to you. The best outcome often appears when your facts line up with your inner sense of what is right. If you cannot get them to line up perfectly, think about which side you trust more and why.

---

17. Setting Markers to Evaluate Progress

When a choice is big and the outcome unfolds over time, it helps to set markers to check how things are going. For example, if you decide to start a small online store, you could set markers at one month, three months, and six months. At each marker, you measure sales, customer feedback, or the time and money you have spent. If things are going better than expected, you might invest more. If things are going worse, you can step back or look for ways to improve.

These markers let you avoid drifting along blindly. You see if the outcome is matching what you hoped. If it is not, you can make changes before the problem grows too big. This approach turns decision-making into an ongoing process, not just a single event.

---

18. Handling Outcomes That Do Not Go Your Way

No matter how carefully you plan, sometimes outcomes fall short of what you wanted. That does not always mean your decision was bad. Life can be random, or events can turn against you despite your best efforts. When this happens, the key is to learn from it. Ask:

- "Which parts of this process went well?"
- "Which parts did I overlook or handle poorly?"
- "If I had the chance to do this again, what would I change?"

By asking these questions, you turn a disappointment into a lesson. That lesson can guide you to better decisions and outcomes in the future. Dwelling on blame or regret does not help. Focusing on growth and understanding does.

---

19. Accepting Imperfect Outcomes

Sometimes, you get an outcome that is not great but also not a total loss. It might be so-so, or you might have mixed feelings about it. That is normal. Not every choice leads to a clear win or lose. At times, it might be a tie with both benefits and drawbacks.

In those cases, look for small positives you can keep. Maybe you gained a valuable skill or made a new friend. Even if things did not turn out as you hoped, those positives can still be stepping stones. By accepting imperfect outcomes, you avoid the trap of always wanting everything to be ideal. Life often lands somewhere between perfect and disastrous.

20. **Putting It All Together**

Thinking about possible outcomes helps you make better decisions by shining a light on the future before you get there. It is not about knowing exactly what will happen—that is impossible. It is about becoming aware of what could happen and planning wisely. By using tools like pros and cons, decision trees, scenario planning, and probability checks, you give yourself a stronger base of knowledge.

Keep in mind that even the most thorough planning cannot remove all risk. You also need flexibility. If something changes or you learn new facts, you might need to adjust. That is part of the process. The more you practice looking ahead, the better you get at spotting hidden twists, seeing chances for success, and steering around big pitfalls. Over time, you will find that mapping possible outcomes gives you more calm and confidence in every choice you face.

Chapter 8: Responding to Sudden Changes

Life can throw surprises at you without warning. A new rule at your job might appear, a family emergency might pop up, or a close friend might move away. In those moments, you have to make decisions fast. It is one thing to plan when you have plenty of time, but sudden changes do not always allow that. This chapter explores how to adapt quickly, keep your cool, and still make thoughtful choices when time is short or when you are dealing with unexpected challenges.

---

1. **Why Sudden Changes Can Be Stressful**

People often like knowing what to expect, so they can plan accordingly. When a sudden change hits, you lose that sense of certainty. It might involve a big shift in plans, a lack of resources you were counting on, or a need to act right now. This can be stressful because you have not had a chance to weigh all your options the way you might prefer.

Furthermore, strong emotions can surge when changes are abrupt. You might feel fear, anger, sadness, or frustration. These feelings can cloud your thinking, making it even harder to act in a calm, logical way. Yet, with the right strategies, you can stay steady enough to handle the situation effectively.

---

2. **Keeping a Level Head Under Pressure**

In moments of sudden change, your first job is to keep calm. If you panic, you risk making a quick choice that could worsen the situation. One way to control panic is through simple grounding techniques:

- **Deep Breathing:** Take a slow breath in through your nose, hold it for a moment, and release it through your mouth. Repeat a few times.
- **Counting:** Silently count backward from 10 or 20 to give your mind a brief pause.
- **Focusing on the Present:** Notice the sights, sounds, or textures around you to anchor yourself in reality.

These brief actions help you settle your nerves and keep your mind clear. Even if you only have a few seconds, that small break can make a big difference in how you handle the next steps.

---

3. **Gathering Quick Facts**

When sudden change hits, you might not have the luxury of in-depth research. Still, you need enough facts to decide. Ask yourself: "What is the most important thing I need to know right now?" For example, if your class schedule is suddenly changed, the key facts might be which new books are needed or which classes you must rearrange. If there is an emergency at home, the key facts might be who is safe, who needs help, and where you can get that help.

If others are involved, ask them concise questions. If a coworker suddenly quits, your manager might know the immediate tasks that need coverage. If a friend cancels a carpool arrangement, you might quickly ask them, "How else can I get to work?" Focus on the facts that matter most at this moment. You can gather more details later if time allows.

---

4. **Prioritizing Urgent Needs**

When everything seems chaotic, it is easy to become overwhelmed. The trick is to identify the top priorities first. Imagine you are in a sudden storm, and your roof starts to leak. Your first move might be to stop the water from pouring in and move important items away from the wet area. You do not need to plan the entire roof repair that moment. The same principle applies to other sudden changes: fix or respond to what is critical first, then handle smaller tasks once you have breathing room.

Write down or list in your head the most urgent tasks. Ask yourself, "If I ignore this for a while, will it cause bigger trouble?" If the answer is yes, that item is high priority. By taking care of those key tasks, you limit damage and set the stage for calmer decision-making later.

---

5. **Staying Flexible**

A big part of dealing with sudden change is staying flexible. Your original plan might no longer work, so you have to adapt. That can mean rethinking your schedule, finding new ways to do a task, or adjusting your goals for the time being. Flexibility does not mean giving up on what you want; it means being willing to find another route if your usual path is blocked.

For instance, if you planned to travel somewhere, but your flight is canceled, you might check for a different airline or consider driving if possible. If a financial issue pops up, you might cut back on non-essential spending. Being flexible can reduce stress because you are not clinging to a plan that no longer fits the new reality.

---

6. **Using a Rapid Brainstorm**

When time is short, a rapid brainstorm can help you quickly see options. Grab a piece of paper or open a quick note on your phone, and list any idea that comes to mind—no matter how odd it seems. Do not judge the ideas yet. The aim is to generate possibilities. After you list them, pick the ones that seem most doable. This process can happen in minutes if needed. It might look like this:

- **Situation:** Your usual babysitter cancels on the day of an important meeting.
- **Brainstorm:** Ask a neighbor, ask a family member, see if the meeting can be moved to virtual, bring your child with you if allowed, reschedule your meeting, look for an emergency babysitter service online.
- **Pick Options to Try First:** Text your neighbor and family to see who is free. If none can help, contact your boss to see if a virtual option is possible.

This quick approach gets you moving forward instead of freezing in panic.

---

7. **Revisiting Your Main Goal**

In a sudden change, it is easy to lose sight of what your main goal was in the first place. Ask, "What am I really trying to achieve?" If you can keep that goal in mind, you can be more creative about how you reach it. For example, if your goal was to complete a group project at school, and one group member suddenly drops out, you can still meet the goal by splitting tasks among the remaining members or asking the teacher to join another group. Focusing on the core goal helps you see that even if some parts of the plan change, the overall aim can remain the same.

---

8. Communicating Clearly with Others

Sudden changes often involve other people, whether it is family, coworkers, or friends. Clear communication is crucial so that misunderstandings do not add to the chaos. Use short, direct statements about what is happening and what you need. If you are upset, try to calm down first so that your words are steady.

You might say, "We had an unexpected problem, and here is what I need from you right now." Or, "Our plan has changed. Let's talk about the best way to move forward." By stating the new situation and the immediate steps, you help everyone adjust faster. If the sudden change affects others, ask for their input too, so they feel heard and can offer solutions.

---

9. Managing Emotional Reactions

Strong emotions can flare up when life shifts without warning. You might feel angry at whoever caused the change, or embarrassed if you feel unprepared, or just sad if you lose something important. These emotions are normal, but you want to handle them so they do not lead you to snap decisions.

Give yourself a moment to acknowledge the emotion: "I feel really frustrated right now." Then decide if you can set it aside until you handle the urgent tasks. Sometimes, you can process the emotion later by talking with a trusted person or writing down your thoughts. The idea is not to ignore your feelings entirely, but to keep them from blocking you when fast action is needed.

10. Short-Term Fix vs. Long-Term Solution

In an urgent situation, you might first go for a quick fix just to stabilize things. For example, if a pipe bursts in your house, you turn off the main water valve to stop flooding. That is the short-term fix. But you still need a plumber to come and properly repair the pipe. When faced with sudden change, it is fine to find a short-term fix to buy time, but do not forget to seek a lasting answer later.

The same logic can apply to unexpected personal or work problems. You might temporarily take on extra tasks for a coworker who quit, but that does not solve the bigger issue of needing a replacement. Keep track of which actions are immediate fixes and which are full solutions. Then, you can move from the quick patch to the lasting remedy once things are stable again.

---

11. Avoiding Rash Choices Out of Fear

When people panic, they sometimes leap to solutions that can cause more trouble. For instance, quitting a job on the spot because of a sudden disagreement can lead to financial stress you did not plan for. While there are cases when a quick exit is needed, ensure you are not just acting out of raw fear. If possible, give yourself a moment to think about the pros and cons, even if it is brief.

Take a step back: "If I choose this, what happens tomorrow, next week, or next month?" If the answer is too scary, you might hold off on that extreme action unless you truly have no better option. Sometimes, waiting just a few hours or a day helps you see that there is a calmer path.

---

12. Accepting Help

Sudden changes can be too big to handle alone. If friends, relatives, or colleagues offer help, think about accepting it. This might mean asking someone to watch your kids while you handle an emergency or asking a coworker to share some tasks. Some people feel embarrassed or proud and do not want to seem weak. But asking for help can be wise and responsible, especially if it prevents bigger issues.

If no one steps forward on their own, do not be shy about reaching out. You can say, "I am in a bind. Is there any chance you can help me with this specific thing?" Being direct and polite often yields a better response than hinting or staying silent. By letting others pitch in, you spread the load so you do not burn out.

---

13. Keeping Track of Changing Details

In a sudden shift, details can change quickly. For example, if you are moving on short notice, the moving truck availability, the new apartment lease, and your schedule might shift several times. Write these updates down or keep them in a note on your phone. Staying organized helps you avoid confusion.

It might help to create a simple checklist. As you complete each urgent step, you mark it off. That way, you know what you have done and what still needs attention. This is crucial when time is tight, because you do not want to waste mental energy trying to remember everything. Once you write it down, you free your mind to focus on problem-solving.

---

14. Keeping Others Updated

If the sudden change affects a group, keep everyone on the same page. For instance, if you are leading a team project at school and the submission date moves forward, let everyone know immediately. Send a brief message summarizing the new deadline and what you need from each person. Staying in sync prevents mix-ups and helps the group adjust together.

This also applies to family situations. If plans for a family event change because of weather, let everyone know right away. The faster you communicate, the less confusion and frustration people experience. Clear, quick updates mean fewer last-minute scrambles for everyone.

---

15. Learning from the Surprise

After you handle a sudden change, take a little time to reflect. Ask, "Why did this catch me off guard?" Sometimes, it was truly beyond your control. But other times, you might see ways to be better prepared next time. Maybe you learn to keep a small emergency fund, to double-check your schedule for potential overlaps, or to keep a list of backup options for babysitters or pet sitters.

By learning from the experience, you can reduce the impact of future surprises. You cannot predict every curveball in life, but you can create buffers and routines that make sudden changes less chaotic. That way, each unexpected event teaches you something about coping.

---

16. Thinking About Future Flexibility

If you notice that life throws sudden changes at you often—maybe because of your job or your family's needs—it might be wise to build more flexibility into your routine. For instance, if your job requires you to be on call, keep a flexible schedule at home so you can handle unexpected shifts. If your family situation is unpredictable, have backup childcare or a rotating plan for chores.

This approach might also mean avoiding overcommitting yourself. If you are booked every minute of the day, a single surprise can make the whole schedule crash. Leaving some open space or free time in your routine can be a cushion to handle last-minute demands.

---

17. Using a Calm Yet Firm Mindset

When a sudden change happens, you want to be calm enough to think clearly, but also firm enough to act without hesitation. This balance can be tricky. One way is to focus on what you know for sure, rather than what is unknown or unconfirmed. You can say, "I know these three facts, so I will base my action on them." You can adjust later if new facts appear.

Being firm does not mean being stubborn. If you find out your initial guess was wrong, be willing to switch tactics. But do not let uncertainty freeze you. You can say, "Based on what I know right now, this is my best move," and then proceed.

18. Keeping a Sense of Perspective

In the heat of the moment, a sudden change can feel like the end of the world. But once the dust settles, you might realize it was not that big in the grand scheme of things. Try to keep perspective by asking: "Will this matter a year from now?" or "Is there still a path forward even if this part changed?" Often, you will see that while the surprise is inconvenient, it does not spell total doom.

This does not mean brushing off serious issues. Some surprises are indeed major, like the loss of a job or a serious health problem. Even then, it helps to remember that people can recover from setbacks with the right support and plan. Keeping a bit of hope and perspective can stop despair from taking over.

---

19. Supporting Others Who Are Affected

You might be the calm person in a sudden change while others around you are scared or confused. Offering them steady guidance can help everyone get through it more smoothly. You could assign tasks, share updates, or simply assure them that things will be okay once you handle the urgent steps.

Remember that some people handle change worse than others. They might be more anxious or less experienced at problem-solving. If you can show patience and kindness, you become a source of stability. Working together often makes it easier to cope with surprises than trying to handle them all by yourself.

---

20. Moving On Once the Crisis Passes

After you manage the sudden shift and things calm down, it is helpful to move forward rather than stay stuck in the crisis mindset. You might still have smaller tasks left, but the biggest threat might be over. Take stock of what you learned:

- **Did you discover a weakness in your plan that you can fix for next time?**
- **Did you see a new opportunity that arose because of the sudden change?**
- **Is there anything you need to change permanently to avoid a repeat problem?**

Once you have answered these questions, shift your focus back to your normal goals and routines. Clinging to the stress of the surprise can drain you. It is healthier to note the lessons, adjust where needed, and continue with your life.

Putting Sudden Changes in Perspective

Sudden changes can be stressful and disruptive, but they do not have to ruin your plans. With rapid fact-gathering, a calm approach, clear communication, and a willingness to adapt, you can often turn a surprise into a workable situation. These moments also teach you how strong and resourceful you can be under pressure. Over time, each surprise you handle makes you more confident in your ability to tackle whatever comes next.

By remembering to pause, breathe, and address urgent tasks first, you set the stage for better decisions. You learn to keep your main goal in sight, speak up when you need help, and avoid rash moves that cause more harm. While no one likes to be thrown off course, you can train yourself to respond wisely. The steps in this chapter show that handling sudden changes is not about being perfect—it is about staying steady, thinking on your feet, and finding the best path forward in unfamiliar territory.

Chapter 9: Asking for Advice and Support

Sometimes, making decisions on your own can feel overwhelming. You might have questions you cannot answer or worries you cannot solve alone. That is when advice and support from others can be a big help. This chapter focuses on how to reach out for helpful input and how to build a network of people you trust. You will learn why it is not a sign of weakness to ask for help, how to find the right people to ask, how to filter the advice you get, and how to support others in return.

1. **Why We Hesitate to Ask for Help**

Many people do not like to ask for advice or support. They might feel shy, worried about looking weak, or afraid of being judged. Some fear that asking for help means they are not smart or capable. In reality, asking for help is a normal part of learning and growing. Nobody knows everything. Even experts often talk to peers to get fresh insights.

If you find yourself hesitating, ask: "Would I think someone else is weak if they asked me for help?" Probably not. In fact, you might respect them for wanting to learn. Keep in mind that most people enjoy being useful. They might be pleased you trust them enough to ask for their view.

2. **Figuring Out What Kind of Support You Need**

Before asking for advice, take a moment to figure out exactly what you need. Are you looking for a solution to a problem? Do you just want someone to listen to your thoughts? Do you need emotional comfort? Clarity on a process? Each of these needs might call for a different person or a different type of help.

For instance, if your decision involves a technical skill, you might turn to a teacher or a professional. If you need a listening ear because you feel stressed, you might turn to a close friend or a family member who is good at offering kindness. By pinpointing the kind of support you need, you raise your chances of getting advice that truly helps.

3. **Choosing Who to Ask**

Picking the right person is important. Not everyone will have the knowledge or the attitude to help you well. Some might make you feel judged. Others might steer you toward what they want instead of what is best for you. Consider these points when choosing someone to ask:

- **Experience**: Do they have useful knowledge about your topic?
- **Trustworthiness**: Can you trust them not to share your private thoughts with others?
- **Open-Mindedness**: Will they listen without pushing their own ideas too hard?
- **Honesty**: Will they tell you the truth rather than just telling you what you want to hear?

A good advisor does not have to be an older person or a professional all the time. Friends, classmates, neighbors, or relatives can also offer sound ideas if they meet the above points.

---

4. **Approaching Mentors and Experts**

If your question is about a certain career path or skill, you might want to seek a mentor or expert. A mentor could be a teacher, a coach, or a person who has done what you hope to do. Their advice can save you time and mistakes. When contacting a mentor, be polite and clear about why you admire them and what you hope to learn.

For example, if you want to ask an experienced computer programmer for advice, you could say, "I respect your coding experience, and I am hoping to improve my programming skills. Would you be willing to share some guidance on what I should practice first?" People often respond well when they see that you have a genuine respect for their expertise.

---

5. **Being Respectful of Other People's Time**

When you ask for support, remember that the person you are asking might be busy. Respect their schedule. If you call or send a message, keep it short. Let them know what you need and why. For example, you might say, "I have a big test coming up next week. Could we talk for fifteen minutes about your study methods?" This approach shows that you value their time, which makes them more likely to help.

If they say they cannot help right now, do not take it personally. They might have other things going on. You can politely ask if there is a better time or if they know someone else who could help. People appreciate it when you give them a graceful way out, rather than pushing them to respond immediately.

---

6. **Asking Clear Questions**

Vague questions lead to vague answers. Try to be as clear as you can about your concern. Instead of saying, "I need help with math," say, "I am struggling with algebra, especially word problems. Could you show me how to break them down step by step?" This level of detail helps the other person know where to start and what kind of answer will help you the most.

If you are not sure exactly what is confusing you, then explain what you do understand and where you start to feel lost. This helps your advisor narrow down the point that needs attention. Clear questions usually get more useful answers.

---

7. **Listening Actively**

Asking for advice is pointless if you do not listen well to the answer. Active listening involves giving your full attention, asking follow-up questions, and rephrasing what the person said to ensure you understood. You might say, "So, if I understand you correctly, you are suggesting I spend an hour each day reviewing my notes. Is that right?" This lets them confirm or correct your understanding.

Active listening also shows the person you respect their time. People offering advice like to know that you are taking their words seriously. If you tune out, they may feel you are wasting both their time and yours, and they will be less willing to help in the future.

8. Handling Conflicting Advice

It is common to get different advice from different people. One person might say, "Take the risk," while another says, "Play it safe." When advice conflicts, do not just pick the one you like better right away. Instead, break down each piece of advice. Ask why each person holds that view. Are they talking from personal experience? Do they have different values from you?

Comparing advice can help you see a situation from many angles. You might blend the best parts of each idea. Or you might decide that one set of advice fits your situation better. The important thing is to avoid confusion by looking at the reasons behind each viewpoint. Then, make your own decision based on what feels right to you.

---

9. Knowing When Not to Take Advice

Sometimes, you will receive advice that is not helpful or that clashes strongly with your beliefs. You do not have to take every suggestion, even if it comes from someone who cares about you. For example, if a friend advises you to do something risky that goes against your core values, you can politely decline. You might say, "Thanks for your thoughts. I respect your opinion, but I feel more comfortable doing it another way."

Learning to say no to advice can be hard, especially if you worry about hurting someone's feelings. Still, it is your life, and you get to decide which advice to follow. Being kind but firm is a good approach. Most people will respect your decision if you handle it calmly.

---

10. Balancing Support and Self-Reliance

Advice is meant to guide you, not to make you dependent on others for every step. After collecting thoughts from different sources, take time to figure out what you think. For instance, if you are learning to play an instrument, you might ask your teacher for tips, watch some online lessons, and get feedback from a friend. In the end, it is still your practice sessions that will bring improvement.

Self-reliance means you trust your ability to apply what you learn. You do not wait for someone to tell you exactly what to do all the time. The best decisions often come from blending outside input with your own ideas, life experiences, and instincts.

---

11. Building a Support Network

Rather than waiting until you are in a crisis, it can be wise to build a network of supportive people ahead of time. This network might include:

- **Close Friends**: They know you well and care about your feelings.
- **Family Members**: They often have a big interest in your success and well-being.
- **Teachers or Coaches**: They have knowledge in specific areas, like academics, sports, or arts.
- **Mentors**: They may guide you over the long haul, not just for one problem.
- **Peers with Similar Goals**: They understand what you are going through and can offer mutual help.

When you have a support network, you know where to turn when you face tough decisions. You can also be a source of help for them in return, strengthening the bonds even more.

---

12. Giving and Receiving Encouragement

Advice is not just about telling people what to do. Sometimes, it is about giving emotional support—letting someone know they have what it takes to succeed. Encouragement can be as simple as saying, "I believe you can handle this," or "You have come so far; do not give up now." When you encourage others, you help them feel confident.

In the same way, you can receive encouragement by letting people know you appreciate their words. If a family member or friend cheers you on, say "thank you" and accept their kind thoughts. This exchange of positive support can ease worries and keep you motivated to move forward with your decisions.

13. **Being Aware of Unhelpful Sources**

Not everyone who offers advice does so from a place of truth or kindness. Some people may have selfish aims. Others might enjoy putting you down. Be careful if you notice these behaviors:

- **They always point out your flaws without offering real solutions.**
- **They push you to do something mainly because it benefits them.**
- **They refuse to listen to your point of view at all.**
- **They become angry or insulting if you do not follow their advice.**

If you spot these patterns, it may be best to limit how much you rely on that person. Instead, seek help from people who are respectful, honest, and truly want what is best for you.

---

14. **Overcoming the Fear of Judgment**

One reason people avoid asking for advice is fear of being judged. They worry others will think they are silly or lazy for not knowing something. In most cases, this fear is bigger in our own mind than in reality. In fact, many people enjoy sharing their knowledge. Think about how you feel when someone asks you how to do something you are good at—you might feel happy to help.

If you do face judgment, remember that says more about them than it does about you. A harsh or mocking response suggests they might not be the best person to ask. Look for a more understanding individual next time.

---

15. **Using Online Sources with Care**

The internet can be a big source of advice, from Q&A websites to social media groups. While this can be handy, be cautious. Not all tips you find online are accurate, and some can be harmful. Look for well-known sources, official websites, or professionals who share their expertise. Read reviews or check credentials if possible.

Also, be wary of letting random strangers influence big decisions in your life. It is fine to see what others say, but also think about whether their situation matches yours. If someone on a forum suggests a plan that feels risky or clashes with your reality, you do not have to follow it. Use online advice as one piece of input, not the whole story.

16. When Professional Help Is Needed

Some issues go beyond everyday advice and need professional support. For example, if you are dealing with strong emotional problems like deep sadness, it might be time to see a counselor or therapist. If you have legal or financial concerns, a trained professional in that area can help you avoid serious mistakes.

Reaching out for professional help is nothing to be ashamed of. It shows you understand the limits of casual advice. A counselor, lawyer, or financial advisor can provide detailed knowledge and solutions that friends and family might not be qualified to give.

17. Keeping Track of Useful Guidance

Over time, you might receive many pieces of advice. Some of it will be great; some might be less helpful. It can be easy to forget who said what or which tip helped you the most. Try writing down useful pointers in a notebook or on your phone. Note who gave it, when, and what problem it solved.

Reviewing this record later can remind you of lessons you learned. It can also show you patterns—maybe you notice that certain people give especially practical advice on work issues, while others are better at emotional support. By seeing these patterns, you can know whom to reach out to depending on the type of challenge you face next.

18. Supporting Others in Return

Support is a two-way street. If someone has helped you, be open to helping them when they need it. Even if they do not directly ask, you can check in on how they are doing. Offer your ear if they look stressed. Suggest ideas if they ask for them.

By giving back, you create an environment where everyone feels comfortable sharing both worries and wins.

Being there for others also builds your own confidence. When you explain something you have learned, you strengthen your understanding of it. Helping someone else might even show you new viewpoints you have never considered before.

---

19. Knowing the Limits of Advice

No matter how good the guidance is, you are still the one who must act. Advice can outline what to do, but it cannot do the work for you. Do not become stuck in a loop of always asking, "What should I do?" without ever taking a step. At some point, you have to move forward and try a method, test a plan, or make a choice.

If you catch yourself constantly seeking more and more opinions, ask, "Am I really looking for advice, or am I afraid to act?" If it is fear, remind yourself that no decision is perfect. You can make an informed choice and adjust later if needed. Accepting some risk is part of making progress.

---

20. Putting It All Together

Asking for advice and support is a healthy sign that you recognize life's complexities. You do not have to carry every worry alone. By deciding what kind of help you need, choosing the right people, and being clear in your requests, you set yourself up to receive guidance that matches your situation. Balancing outside help with your own judgment is key, ensuring you grow stronger and more independent along the way.

Remember that you do not need to say yes to every suggestion. It is your life, and you are in control of which advice to follow. Good support can lighten your load, clarify your thinking, and give you fresh ideas. In return, offer a friendly ear or your own knowledge when others come to you. This cycle of asking and giving can enrich your decision-making skills and create a community of trust and respect.

Chapter 10: Using Simple Checklists and Tools

Making decisions can seem complicated when you have multiple tasks, details, and deadlines swirling in your mind. Simple checklists and tools can help you organize your thoughts and approach decisions more systematically. This chapter introduces easy methods that prevent you from forgetting steps, keep your mind focused, and make tasks feel less overwhelming. You will learn how to form checklists that match your needs, explore basic tools for problem-solving, and apply them to everyday situations.

1. Why Checklists Are Helpful

A checklist is basically a list of tasks or steps that you can mark off once done. While it sounds basic, checklists can greatly reduce errors. For example, airplane pilots use pre-flight checklists to ensure they do not miss crucial steps. Nurses and doctors often use checklists to improve patient safety. In daily life, you can use them for chores, school assignments, packing for a trip, and many other tasks.

Checklists help you keep track of details without relying on memory alone. This frees your mind to focus on problem-solving instead of recalling small tasks. They also give you a simple way to see your progress. Each time you mark off a completed task, you get a small sense of relief and motivation to move forward.

2. Creating a Basic Checklist

Making a checklist is simple. First, write down every task you need to do or every step involved in your decision-making process. For example, if you are deciding whether to take an advanced class, your checklist might include steps like:

1. Look at the course syllabus.
2. Talk to the teacher.
3. See how it fits your schedule.
4. Check if it impacts your other activities.
5. Talk to peers who took the class before.
6. Compare pros and cons.

7. Decide if you will enroll.

As you complete each step, put a check next to it or cross it out. A basic paper list or a digital note on your phone can work fine. The goal is to keep it visible so you do not forget where you are in the process.

---

3. Breaking Large Tasks into Smaller Steps

One reason decisions can feel big is that they include many smaller tasks. Trying to tackle them all at once is stressful. Checklists let you break these tasks into bite-size pieces. If you want to switch to a new place to live, for example, you could list out:

1. Research neighborhoods.
2. Check rental or housing prices.
3. Arrange visits to potential places.
4. Compare each place's pros and cons.
5. Talk with a roommate or family member about costs.
6. Make a final choice and sign paperwork.

By seeing each step on paper, you feel less overwhelmed. As you finish one step, you move to the next. It is a clear path that keeps you on track.

---

4. Using Timelines and Calendars

Sometimes, decisions or tasks have deadlines. In that case, a simple timeline or calendar can be a powerful tool. You do not need fancy software—an old-fashioned paper calendar or a digital calendar app both work. Mark important dates, such as when you need to sign documents, when you must have certain paperwork done, or when you should inform someone of your choice.

Putting tasks on a calendar helps you see how much time you really have. You might discover you need to start certain steps earlier or that you have more free days than you expected. This prevents last-minute stress. You can also create reminders or alerts to prompt you before a deadline arrives.

5. **Using Mind Maps for Ideas**

A mind map is a diagram that helps you sort thoughts around a central topic. You write the main idea in the middle, then draw branches for related points, and smaller branches for details. For instance, if you are thinking about studying abroad, you could put "Study Abroad" in the center. Then, branches could include "Cost," "School Options," "Language Requirements," "Housing," and "Culture." Under each branch, list details or tasks.

Mind maps can be drawn on paper or created with a simple computer tool. They are especially useful if you like to see how concepts link together. Instead of a linear list, a mind map gives you a more visual approach. This can help you spot connections you might miss otherwise.

---

6. **Applying Flowcharts to Decision Steps**

Flowcharts can be useful when you have choices that lead to different paths. You start with a shape that states your question. Then, for each choice, you draw arrows branching out. Each arrow can lead to another question or a final result. For a simple example:

- **Box 1**: "Should I buy a used car?"
    - **Arrow 1**: "Yes"
        - Leads to another box: "Check budget."
        - Next arrow: "Do I have enough for it?"
            - If yes, go to "Complete purchase."
            - If no, go to "Look for cheaper option or wait."
    - **Arrow 2**: "No"
        - Ends with "Keep current mode of transport."

Flowcharts help you see the logic behind each decision path. They reduce confusion by showing a step-by-step map of what happens if you say yes or no at any point.

---

7. **Using Simple Spreadsheet Tools**

A spreadsheet can be a helpful way to compare options side by side. Let's say you are choosing between four potential colleges. You can make columns for each college and rows for things like tuition cost, distance from home, size of classes, dorm quality, or sports programs. Then fill in each box with the facts you find. You might also color-code them (like green for good, yellow for okay, and red for poor) to see which college stands out.

Spreadsheets can also help you track budgets. You list income in one column and expenses in another. By summing them, you see if you are spending more than you earn. This kind of organized approach makes decision-making clearer, because all the data is in front of you in an orderly layout.

---

8. **Setting Up "If-Then" Plans**

An "if-then" plan can help you handle unexpected changes or potential obstacles. You list a trigger ("if this happens") and a response ("then I will do this"). For example:

- **If** my car breaks down, **then** I will use public transportation for a week.
- **If** I cannot reach my first-choice college, **then** I will enroll in my second choice and try again next year.
- **If** the price of a certain item is too high, **then** I will wait for a discount or pick an alternative.

This approach takes some of the guesswork out of decisions when surprises come. It also lowers stress because you already have a plan for problems that could appear.

---

9. **Using Prioritization Tools**

When you have a lot of tasks competing for your time, deciding what to do first can be tricky. One easy tool is the "Eisenhower Matrix," which splits tasks into four squares:

- **Important and Urgent**: Do these tasks first.

- **Important but Not Urgent**: Schedule a time to do these.
- **Not Important but Urgent**: If possible, delegate these tasks or handle them quickly so they do not distract you.
- **Not Important and Not Urgent**: These might be dropped or done only after everything else.

By sorting your tasks into these categories, you see which ones deserve your immediate focus. It can prevent you from wasting time on small tasks while ignoring bigger priorities.

---

10. Keeping Notes on Progress

A checklist is only useful if you remember to update it. Try keeping a simple log or note about your daily progress. This can be a short record of what you completed, what obstacles came up, and what the next step is. If you are using a digital tool, you can edit tasks as you go. If you prefer paper, cross off tasks or write the date you finished them.

Reviewing your notes can help you see if you are moving forward at a good pace or if you are falling behind. It also reveals patterns—maybe you notice you always put off certain tasks until the last minute. That clue tells you what to work on improving.

---

11. Staying Flexible with Tools

Checklists and other tools are meant to serve you, not the other way around. If you find that a certain method feels awkward, try a different one. Some people love mind maps, while others prefer linear lists. Some want digital apps with reminders, while others like the feel of writing things down on paper. The key is to find tools that fit your style and help you stay on track.

Feel free to combine methods. You might create a checklist for everyday tasks but use a mind map for bigger decisions. You could keep an "if-then" plan in your phone for quick reference, and also have a flowchart for a project at work. Adapt the tools so they truly help you, rather than forcing yourself to follow a method that does not fit your thinking.

12. Simplifying Complex Data

When you have a lot of information—like dozens of facts about different universities or job options—it can feel overwhelming. One method to simplify is to pick a few key factors that matter most to you. For instance, if you care most about location, cost, and future job openings, focus on those three when comparing. That does not mean other details do not matter, but it can help you narrow down your search.

You can also rate each option on a scale of 1 to 5 for each factor. For example, College A might get a 4 for location, 3 for cost, and 5 for job openings, totaling 12 points. College B might get a 5, 4, and 3, totaling 12 as well. If the totals are the same, look for a smaller detail that might be the tiebreaker. This is not a perfect system, but it is a quick way to see which choices might be stronger for your priorities.

---

13. Avoiding "Tool Overload"

With so many apps, planners, and templates out there, you might feel tempted to use everything at once. This can backfire if you spend more time managing your tools than actually making decisions or doing tasks. Keep it simple. Often, a basic paper list or one good app is enough for everyday needs.

Use new tools only if they solve a real problem. For instance, if you forget tasks because you do not have a good reminder system, an app that sends you alerts can be helpful. But if you already have a planner that works, you do not need a second or third one. Choose the tools that fit your routine, and be careful not to overload yourself with fancy features that are not really needed.

---

14. Checking Off Steps for Motivation

One nice thing about a checklist is the small boost of satisfaction each time you check off a completed step. This feeling can keep you moving when you face tasks that are not exciting. You might even reward yourself in a small way. For example, after finishing five tasks on your list, you might take a quick break to do something relaxing.

This reward does not have to be big or costly. It can be as simple as enjoying a cup of tea, listening to a favorite song, or reading a funny comic. Knowing you will have a mini-break after a set number of tasks can push you to stay focused and get things done.

---

15. Handling Group Tasks

If you are working with a group—whether for a school project or a work assignment—checklists can help everyone coordinate. You can create a shared list with each member's tasks. That way, everyone sees who is responsible for each part. If someone finishes early, they might help a teammate who is struggling.

This open approach also lowers the chance of confusion, like two people doing the same task while another task goes undone. With a group checklist, you can hold each other accountable, ask for updates, and spot delays before they turn into bigger problems. It also creates a sense of teamwork as you see tasks being checked off one by one.

---

16. Making Time for Reflection

After you complete a set of tasks, pause and reflect. Did your checklist help you reach your goal smoothly, or did you run into problems? If there were issues, try adjusting your list for next time. Maybe you needed to break a big step into smaller ones, or you found that certain steps were not needed at all.

Reflection also helps you spot your strengths. You might find that you are very good at quickly finishing tasks that have clear steps. Or you might see that certain tasks always slow you down because you do not enjoy them. Knowing these details lets you plan better in the future, either by changing your approach or seeking help in those weak areas.

---

17. Adapting Tools to Different Life Areas

Checklists and other simple methods are not just for school or work. You can use them for personal goals, like improving your health, planning a party, or tracking hobbies. For example, if you want to cook more meals at home, you could make a weekly menu list and a grocery checklist. If you are planning an event, you could list tasks like booking a space, preparing invitations, arranging snacks, and sorting out music.

Adapting these tools to many areas of life gives you a sense of control. Instead of juggling tasks in your head, you place them on paper or in an app. This lowers mental stress and reduces the chance of forgetting something important.

---

18. Combining Tools for Big Decisions

When facing a very big decision—such as changing careers or making a large purchase—you might use several tools at once:

- **Checklist**: Outlining the steps you need, like researching, budgeting, and consulting a mentor.
- **Spreadsheet**: Comparing different options side by side with cost, benefits, and potential risks.
- **Mind Map**: Brainstorming ideas and concerns around this big life change.
- **Calendar**: Marking deadlines or target dates to decide, so you do not drag out the process forever.

Bringing these tools together helps ensure you do not miss crucial angles. You still want to stay flexible. If you notice you are bogged down in details, step back and see what is truly essential.

---

19. Staying Organized in the Long Run

Decision-making is not a one-time task. Life keeps moving, and new choices appear. Staying organized over the long run can keep stress in check. You might develop a habit of writing a daily to-do list each morning or setting aside time each week to update your personal planner. Over time, these small habits build a foundation that helps you face bigger decisions more calmly.

Consider doing a quick weekly review: look at what you finished, what you still need to do, and what challenges might pop up. This check-in can take as little as ten minutes and can save you from unpleasant surprises later.

20. The Power of Simple Tools

Simple does not mean weak. On the contrary, checklists and basic organizing tools have helped people make better decisions for ages. By breaking tasks down, setting clear steps, and storing facts in an orderly way, you give your mind more space to think creatively about solutions. You also lower the risk of forgetting a key detail.

Whether you use paper or digital methods, the principle is the same: keep track of what needs to be done, check things off, and adapt as necessary. When decisions arise, you will find that you are less scattered and more confident about how to proceed.

Remember, these tools are meant to assist you, not to trap you. If a list or method stops working, you can adjust it. The end goal is to make decisions that match your values and aims, without being overwhelmed by cluttered thoughts. When you see how much calmer it can be to follow a simple plan, you might wonder how you ever managed without one.

Closing Thoughts on Using Checklists and Tools

Checklists, calendars, mind maps, and spreadsheets are plain ways to bring order to the decision-making process. They help you see tasks clearly, focus on what is important, and keep track of progress. While no tool is perfect for everyone, trying out these methods can reveal what works best for your style.

Over time, you might develop a personal mix—maybe a paper planner for daily chores, a spreadsheet for big financial choices, and a mind map for brainstorming creative projects. The key is to stay flexible and adapt. Life changes, and so can your system. By learning to use these tools well, you give yourself a clear head and a more relaxed approach to making choices, big or small.

Chapter 11: Avoiding Common Traps

When making decisions, many people slip into traps that they do not even notice at first. These traps can cause confusion, extra costs, or missed chances. Some traps come from how our mind works, while others appear because of social or environmental influences. By learning about these traps, you can recognize them early and steer around them. This chapter will look at frequent traps, explain why they happen, and give ideas on how to avoid them.

The Overconfidence Trap
Overconfidence means believing you know more or can do more than is realistic. It can make you guess wrong about your chance of success or how easy a choice will be. For example, you might decide to enter a talent contest without practicing much, thinking, "I am sure I will do fine," and end up unprepared. Or you might invest money in a risky idea because you trust your gut far more than facts.

- **Why It Happens**: Sometimes, past successes make you think you will always do well. Other times, you might not see your own limits or want to impress yourself or others.
- **How to Avoid It**: Ask yourself, "What facts do I have to back up my plan?" Check if you are ignoring negative signs. It also helps to ask a trusted friend or mentor for an honest opinion. They can point out things you might be missing.

The All-or-Nothing Trap
This trap involves seeing choices in black-and-white terms with no middle ground. You might think, "If I cannot do it perfectly, I will not do it at all," or, "I have to succeed on the first try or it means I am a failure." Such rigid thinking can keep you from taking small steps that lead to better results over time.

- **Why It Happens**: Fear of mistakes or fear of not reaching a high standard can make you see only extremes.
- **How to Avoid It**: Remind yourself that partial success or steady progress is still worthwhile. Set modest steps instead of demanding perfection right away. If you do well, great. If not, you can adjust and keep going.

The Sunk Cost Trap

The sunk cost trap is when you keep pouring effort, time, or money into something simply because you have already invested a lot, even if it no longer makes sense. For instance, you might keep attending a club you no longer enjoy because you spent money on the membership. Or you might keep fixing a very old car when buying a newer one would be cheaper in the long run.

- **Why It Happens**: People dislike the thought of "wasting" what they have already spent. They also get attached to their choices and do not want to admit it might have been a poor decision.
- **How to Avoid It**: Focus on the future. Ask, "If I had not put anything into this yet, would I start now?" If the answer is no, it is a sign you might be better off letting go. Do not feel guilty about stepping away. It is more wasteful to keep sinking resources into a lost cause.

The Confirmation Trap

This trap involves looking only for information that agrees with what you already think, while ignoring facts that go against it. Say you believe a certain food is unhealthy. You might read blogs that confirm this idea and skip those that say it can be okay in moderation. As a result, you form a one-sided view and might make a flawed decision based on partial information.

- **Why It Happens**: People feel more comfortable when their beliefs are reinforced. It is unpleasant to see you might have been wrong.
- **How to Avoid It**: Try actively looking for the opposite point of view. Talk to people who disagree with you. See if you can find valid arguments on both sides. When you consider all angles, you make a more balanced choice.

The "Shiny Object" Trap

This trap happens when something new and exciting draws your attention, causing you to drop your current plans. For example, you might give up on a business idea that is going well because a newer concept looks more fun. Or you might buy a brand-new gadget you do not really need because advertisements make it look flashy.

- **Why It Happens**: Novelty can be tempting. We like fresh experiences, and we may worry we are missing out on something better.
- **How to Avoid It**: Ask yourself, "What do I gain if I switch now?" or, "Will this distract me from a path that is already working?" If the new thing truly offers more benefits than your current plan, that is fine. But be cautious if you keep changing directions for no solid reason.

The Blame Trap

In the blame trap, you pin the results of your decisions on others instead of accepting your own part. You might blame parents for not teaching you certain skills or blame friends for giving poor advice. While others can affect your choices, focusing only on blame can prevent you from learning and improving.

- **Why It Happens**: It is often easier to find a scapegoat than to look at your role in the outcome. We do not want to feel responsible for failures.
- **How to Avoid It**: Recognize your part in each decision, whether good or bad. Think, "What could I do differently next time?" Even if others had a part, you can still gain lessons by looking at what you can control—your actions and responses.

The "I Must Hurry" Trap

Feeling rushed can lead to big mistakes. You might jump to the fastest option without checking if it meets your real needs. A classic example is signing a contract without reading the fine print because the offer "ends today."

- **Why It Happens**: People do not like losing deals or missing deadlines. Companies or individuals might purposely create a sense of urgency to push you.
- **How to Avoid It**: Pause and ask, "Is this deadline real, or can I ask for extra time?" If it is truly urgent, set aside a short moment to do a quick check of the important details. If it is not urgent, give yourself enough space to think.

The Comparison Trap

In the comparison trap, you base your decisions too much on what others do. You might see your peers buying expensive clothes, so you do the same even if you cannot afford it. Or you might see a friend take a certain job and assume you must do something similar.

- **Why It Happens**: Social influence is strong. We often want to keep up with friends or follow the crowd.
- **How to Avoid It**: Focus on your own resources, needs, and values. Ask, "Would I still want this if nobody else had it?" or, "Does this help my life, or am I just copying others?" By being honest, you can avoid decisions that do not truly fit you.

The Comfort Trap
The comfort trap occurs when you keep picking what is safe or normal, even if it limits better opportunities. You might stay in a job you do not like for years because it is familiar, or avoid meeting new people because you feel shy. Over time, this stops you from growing and making bold but beneficial moves.

- **Why It Happens**: Stepping out of the familiar can be scary. You might fear failure, social awkwardness, or extra work.
- **How to Avoid It**: Make small experiments to see if trying something new could actually bring good results. Start with low-stakes changes, like learning a small new skill, and see that not all change leads to bad outcomes. With practice, you can get used to minor discomfort for a bigger gain.

The "All Talk, No Action" Trap
Talking about goals and plans can feel good, but action is what counts. This trap involves spending a lot of time planning, discussing, or dreaming, yet never taking the first step. You might tell friends, "I want to start a side job," or, "I am going to get in shape," but keep doing nothing for weeks or months.

- **Why It Happens**: Talking about plans can bring a sense of progress without real effort. There might also be fear of failure or not knowing where to begin.
- **How to Avoid It**: Whenever you catch yourself just talking, ask, "What is one small thing I can do right now?" It could be sending an email, making a phone call, or setting up a quick budget. Action can be small, but it must be real.

The "I Should Please Everyone" Trap
Trying to make everyone happy can lead to choices that do not serve your own

well-being. You might take on tasks you hate or follow a path your relatives prefer, even if it clashes with your personal aims. Over time, you feel drained and might blame others for your dissatisfaction.

- **Why It Happens**: We often want approval or fear upsetting people. Some cultures place strong importance on group harmony.
- **How to Avoid It**: Recognize you have a right to your own direction. Kindly but firmly set limits. This does not mean ignoring others' feelings, but it does mean balancing their needs with your own.

The Information Overload Trap

You might research a topic so deeply that you never decide because you keep finding more data to read. This trap can leave you stuck, as you always think "I need one more piece of info." Meanwhile, time passes, and you miss the best window to act.

- **Why It Happens**: Fear of making a wrong choice can push you to gather as many details as possible. You might also enjoy reading and get sidetracked.
- **How to Avoid It**: Set a limit on how much time or how many sources you will check. After that, weigh what you have found and make a choice. You can adjust later if new facts come up, but do not remain stuck forever in research mode.

The Label Trap

This trap involves putting yourself into a box like, "I am just not good at math," or, "I am shy, so I cannot speak in public." Such labels can keep you from trying new approaches. You end up ignoring the fact that skills can improve and personalities can adapt.

- **Why It Happens**: Negative experiences or remarks from others can make you think you are limited. It feels safer to accept that label rather than risk failing.
- **How to Avoid It**: Treat any label as something that can change with effort or practice. If you think you are bad at math, seek a tutor or use a new study method. If you feel shy, take small steps to speak up in safe settings. You might be surprised how much you can grow.

The One-Size-Fits-All Trap

This trap means assuming that a method that worked for someone else must also work for you. For example, a friend might say they studied for an exam by pulling an all-nighter, so you decide to do the same without looking at your own study style. Or a coworker suggests a diet plan that helped them, and you try it blindly even if your body or budget is different.

- **Why It Happens**: We see success stories and want the same results, but forget each person's situation can differ.
- **How to Avoid It**: View other people's methods as examples, not rules. Adapt them to your life. Test things in small ways first to see if they suit you. If they do not, adjust or look for another approach.

The Fear-of-Missing-Out Trap

Fear of missing out can make you accept invites or tasks you do not really want because you imagine something great will happen without you. You might keep your schedule overloaded just in case something exciting occurs. This can spread you too thin and rob you of focus.

- **Why It Happens**: We do not like the idea of being left out or losing a chance at fun, profit, or social bonding.
- **How to Avoid It**: Ask if the activity truly fits your goals or personal style. You cannot do everything. Missing out on some events is part of life. If you keep your focus on what actually matters to you, you reduce the pull of pointless distractions.

The Instant Gratification Trap

This trap involves picking what feels good right now over what is better in the future. For instance, you might spend your savings on a fancy gadget instead of keeping it for tuition fees. Or you might skip studying to watch videos because studying feels less fun in the present moment.

- **Why It Happens**: Human brains often like quick rewards. We do not always focus on future effects.
- **How to Avoid It**: Think about how you might feel later if you choose the short-term reward over the long-term gain. If the long-term benefit is important enough, remind yourself that the short-term reward will not be worth the regret you might feel down the line.

The "Not My Fault" Trap

This is a bit like the blame trap but focuses more on ignoring personal responsibility. You might think every negative outcome happens because of outside forces—bad luck, tough rules, or unhelpful people. While external factors do matter, this mindset keeps you from seeing what you can change.

- **Why It Happens**: Admitting some decisions are within your control can be scary. Accepting responsibility means you cannot just shrug off mistakes.
- **How to Avoid It**: Start small. Ask, "What part of this situation can I control?" Even if it is a small part, working on that area can improve results. Accept that luck and other factors exist, but your actions do count.

The "Low Energy" Trap

This trap pops up when you are too tired or stressed to think clearly, so you pick the easiest option without comparing. For example, you might be exhausted after work and decide on a big purchase online just because it is fast to click "buy," not because it is the best deal.

- **Why It Happens**: Fatigue lowers our ability to think deeply. Stress can make us want quick relief.
- **How to Avoid It**: Do important decision-making when you are rested. If you feel drained, try to wait until you can have a clear mind. A short break, a nap, or a snack can sometimes help you regain enough energy to think properly.

The "No Reflection" Trap

After you pick a path and get results—good or bad—you might move on without looking back. This means you miss the chance to learn from what happened. You repeat the same mistakes or do not note the helpful steps that led to success.

- **Why It Happens**: People are busy. Also, reflecting might force us to see our errors or missed hints.
- **How to Avoid It**: Build a habit of checking in after each big decision. Ask, "What went right? What went wrong? What would I do differently next time?" Write short notes if it helps you remember. Over time, you can see patterns in your behavior and adjust.

Practical Ways to Steer Clear of Traps

- **Use Reminders**: Sticky notes, alarms, or a planner app can prompt you to double-check your reasoning before making a choice.

- **Ask "What If?"**: Imagine outcomes for each option. If you see an obvious pitfall, you might be heading for a trap.
- **Get Outside Opinions**: A fresh set of eyes can catch biases or limited thinking.
- **Slow Down**: When possible, do not rush. Even a few extra minutes can help you see if a trap is looming.
- **Test on a Small Scale**: Before committing fully, do a trial run or a smaller test of the idea. This reveals if you are on the wrong path.

Wrapping Up Chapter 11

Common traps appear in many forms—overconfidence, fear, blame, and more. Most of these traps sneak in because of how we think or because we do not want to face certain facts. The bright side is that once you know these traps, you can look for their warning signs. Learning to question yourself gently, gather balanced facts, and step away from extremes can keep you on a more solid path. You will not always avoid every trap, but with practice, you will sidestep many of them and handle your decisions more wisely.

By keeping an eye out for these pitfalls, you gain more control over your actions. You are less likely to waste time or resources, and you can make clearer, stronger decisions. In the next chapter, you will learn about defining clear targets, which helps you pick where you want to go instead of stumbling around these traps without direction.

Chapter 12: Defining Clear Targets

Having a clear target gives you a direction. When you know exactly what you want to achieve, it is much simpler to judge if a choice fits that aim or not. Without a defined target, you may feel scattered or unsure why you are making certain decisions. This chapter will talk about how to shape your targets so they guide you in a strong, concrete way. By knowing your own targets, you can focus your efforts, measure your progress, and make decisions that get you closer to what you want.

Why Clear Targets Matter

A target is a goal or outcome you want to reach. For example, finishing a big project, saving money to buy something important, or improving your skill in a sport. When your target is fuzzy, it is easy to drift. You might waste energy on random tasks that do not help you. You also will not know if you are getting closer to success.

On the other hand, a clear target acts like a compass. Each time you face a choice—big or small—you can ask, "Will this move me closer to my target?" If yes, you might go ahead. If no, you might skip it or do it later. Clarity also helps you feel more purposeful and motivated because you see a meaningful reason behind your tasks.

Being Specific

Specific targets are easier to handle than vague ones. Saying, "I want to be healthier" sounds nice, but it is so broad that you might not know where to start. A clearer version might be, "I want to walk for 30 minutes, four days a week, and limit junk food to two times a week." Now you have clear actions. You also know exactly what success looks like—if you do those tasks, you meet your target.

If your target is about learning something, you could say, "I will read two chapters of a coding book each week and practice for one hour every weekend." That is more specific than "I want to learn to code." It gives you a clear outline of what to do.

Making Targets Measurable

If you can measure your target, you can track progress. For instance, if you plan to save money, set an exact figure, like "I want to save $500 by the end of the year." That way, you can see each week or month how much you have saved so far. If you see you are at $300 by the middle of the year, you know you are on track.

Measurable targets work well because the numbers do not lie. If your aim is to study 10 new vocabulary words each day, you can count them. If your aim is to reduce your online screen time to 2 hours a day, you can check your device usage. This clarity helps you see growth and spot problems faster.

Checking That Targets Are Doable

Sometimes people set very big targets that are not realistic for their current situation. For instance, deciding to run a marathon in two weeks when you have never run before is likely too big a stretch. This can lead to failure and frustration, which might make you give up. A more reasonable target might be to run a shorter distance or to train gradually over a few months.

A doable target should stretch you but not break you. If you are not sure, you can start with smaller steps and increase them if you see you are doing well. For example, if your long-term target is to learn a new language, you might start with a plan to study 20 minutes a day. Once that feels easy, you could increase to 30 or 40 minutes.

Linking Targets to Personal Values

A target that connects with what you truly care about will be more motivating. If you value creativity, a target about painting two pictures a month might inspire you. If you value helping others, a target about volunteering at a local group might excite you. On the other hand, if you set a target just because someone else told you to do it, you might not feel a personal drive to stick with it.

When picking a target, ask yourself, "Why does this matter to me?" If the only reason is external pressure, it might not stick. But if it speaks to your own values or interests, you are more likely to find the energy to continue, even when tasks become hard.

Breaking Big Targets into Phases

A big goal, like writing a 200-page book or mastering an advanced skill, can feel overwhelming if you look at it as one giant task. Breaking it into smaller phases makes it less scary. For instance, aim to write a certain number of pages each week, or to learn a piece of a skill each month. Each step is like a mini-target that moves you forward.

Phases also help you see progress. You get to say, "I finished phase one—good job," which can keep your motivation up. It is much easier to stay engaged when you have frequent signs of movement rather than waiting a long time to see any result.

Attaching Timelines to Targets

It is helpful to pick a finish date or a check-in date for your targets. Otherwise, you might keep pushing them off. For example, if your target is to tidy your entire home, you could decide that by the last day of next month, you want each room to be organized. Then, you can divide the tasks by week or day. Having a clear timeline prompts you to start now rather than "later."
Timelines also help you measure if you are on track. If you are halfway through the time you set and nowhere near halfway done, that is a sign you need to speed up or adjust your plan. If you are ahead of schedule, you might set an even stronger target next time.

Writing Targets Down

Putting your target in writing gives it a more serious feel. You can place a note somewhere you will see it daily, like on your desk, on your fridge, or in a digital reminder. Each time you see it, you recall your aim. This simple practice helps you stay focused instead of forgetting or postponing.
A physical or digital note also lets you track small wins. You can mark each time you complete a step. This steady feedback keeps you from drifting off course. It can be as easy as writing your target at the top of a page and listing daily or weekly actions below.

Staying Flexible When Needed

Even the best targets might need tweaks if life changes. For example, maybe you aimed to read one book a month, but a busy period at work or school uses up your reading time. Instead of quitting, you might adjust your target to one book every two months until life calms down. The main point is to keep moving forward rather than giving up completely.
Staying flexible does not mean you lose discipline. It means you adapt so that your targets still fit reality. If you fall behind on your plan, do not see it as total failure. Instead, revise your timeline or reduce the pace slightly, then keep going. Progress can still happen even if it is slower than you first expected.

Linking Targets to Daily Habits

A target is easier to reach if you turn part of it into a habit. Habits are actions you do often without much thought, like brushing your teeth or checking your phone messages. If you can transform a crucial step toward your target into a habit, you build steady momentum.

For example, if your target is to learn the piano, you can form a habit of practicing for 20 minutes each morning. After a few weeks, it might feel odd not to practice. This consistent routine helps you progress without struggling every day over whether or not to practice. You simply do it because it is part of your day.

Identifying Possible Obstacles
When you define a target, think about what might get in your way. If your target is to exercise three times a week, obstacles might include a busy schedule or feeling too tired after work. If your target is to reduce sugar, you might struggle with cravings or a home that is full of sweet snacks.

Once you know possible obstacles, plan how to handle them. If busy evenings block your workout, maybe you can exercise early in the morning or at lunchtime. If sweet treats tempt you, stock up on healthier snacks or keep fewer sugary items around. By facing these problems in advance, you lower your risk of giving up when they appear.

Rewarding Yourself
While you do not need big prizes, small rewards can help you keep going. You might allow yourself a bit of free time doing something you love after hitting a milestone. Or you might treat yourself to something modest but enjoyable. These rewards mark your progress in a fun way and keep your morale high.

The key is to pick rewards that do not harm your target. For example, if you are trying to save money, do not make your reward a costly item that sets you back. If your target is improving your health, do not make your reward a huge amount of junk food. Find something that feels good but stays in line with your overall aim.

Tracking and Reviewing
Once you set a target, track how you are doing and review it often. This can be a weekly or monthly check-in. Ask:

- "Did I follow my plan this week?"
- "What went well? What was hard?"
- "Do I need to adjust anything?"

By asking these questions, you see where you are succeeding and where you need to make changes. Tracking could be writing in a journal, filling a chart, or using an app that logs your actions. The important part is staying aware of your progress so you do not wake up one day and realize you have gone off track for weeks.

Combining Multiple Targets Carefully

You might have more than one target at a time, like studying for better grades, improving physical fitness, and saving money. Be careful not to overload yourself. Spreading your energy too thin can lead to stress or poor results across all targets.

One approach is to arrange your targets in order of priority. Which one matters most right now? You might give that one the biggest portion of your effort. Alternatively, if two targets do not clash (like reading more books and improving cooking skills), you can schedule them at different times of the day or week. Try to avoid tackling too many tough targets at once, as that could leave you burned out.

Telling Others About Your Target

Sharing your target with a friend or family member can create a sense of accountability. For example, if you announce, "I plan to run a 5K race in three months," your friends might ask you how your training is going. This can encourage you to stick to it, since you do not want to say, "I gave up."

However, be selective about whom you tell. A supportive person can cheer you on. Someone who likes to tease or be negative might discourage you. Choose a person or group that can keep you motivated and remind you of the value in your target.

Staying Motivated in the Middle Phase

Many people are excited when they first set a target, but enthusiasm can dip in the middle. The initial excitement wears off, and the finish line might still be far away. This is a normal phase. The solution is to keep reminding yourself why the target matters. Reflect on the progress you have already made, and picture how good it will feel to reach the end.

You can also break the target into smaller bits so you have more frequent wins. If you are halfway through a language course, celebrate finishing each lesson (just be sure your "celebration" does not clash with any other aims you have). Seeing each small success can keep the spark alive in the middle stretch.

Learning to Adapt
Sometimes your target might change because your life changes. Suppose you aimed to get a certain certificate for a job field, but that field no longer interests you or the job market has shifted. If your aim no longer aligns with your priorities, it can be wise to revise or replace it. That is not the same as failing; it is adjusting to new information or personal growth.

The important thing is to be honest with yourself. Are you giving up just because it is tough, or has your direction truly shifted? If it is just difficulty, you might find ways to overcome the hurdles. If your direction has genuinely changed, allow yourself to form a new target that fits who you are now.

Seeing the Big Picture
Targets do not exist in isolation. They shape how you manage your time, money, and energy. If your target is big—like changing a career path—it might affect your family, your home life, and more. Look at the bigger picture to ensure your target fits into your overall responsibilities and personal values. If you see major conflicts, talk them out with those who might be affected.

For example, if you decide to go back to school full-time, will that clash with other responsibilities or goals you have at home or work? Thinking ahead about these matters helps you plan better and avoid unpleasant surprises.

Recognizing Progress, Even If It Is Small
Sometimes progress is slow and easy to miss. Maybe you are learning a new skill and cannot see big improvements daily. This can be discouraging. One way to stay positive is to focus on small signs of growth. Did you learn a new phrase in a language? Did you run a bit farther this week than last week? Did you manage your budget slightly better this month?

These small steps add up, even if you do not see dramatic changes overnight. Remind yourself that most major changes come from consistent, small efforts. When you look back over a month or two, you may be surprised how far you have come.

Keeping Targets Fresh
Once you complete a target, you might feel a bit lost if you do not have a new

one. That is because setting and working toward targets can give you a sense of direction. When you reach one goal, think about whether you want to take it further or if there is another skill or area you want to explore. This does not mean you must always have huge goals, but it can be nice to keep some form of direction for personal or professional growth.

You can also freshen your existing targets if they have become dull. Maybe you want a different approach or a new challenge to keep your mind engaged. Stale targets can feel like chores, so adding a twist—like finding a study partner or shifting to a more exciting exercise routine—can reignite your interest.

Wrapping Up Chapter 12
Defining clear targets is like setting up a road map for your decisions. With a specific, measurable, and realistic target, you are more likely to move steadily in the right direction. You avoid drifting, wasting time, or forgetting what you hoped to achieve. By linking your targets to your own interests, breaking them into smaller tasks, and tracking your progress, you create a system that supports success.

Also remember that targets are not set in stone. Life can change, or you might discover new things about yourself that guide you to rewrite or refine your aims. That is natural and can keep you from pouring energy into goals that no longer fit. The main idea is to keep some shape and focus in your life—whether it is for a short-term plan, a skill you want to pick up, or a long-term vision.

With clear targets, each choice becomes easier to evaluate. You can simply ask if it leads you closer to your target or not. As you practice setting and meeting targets, you will grow more confident in your ability to manage your path forward. This confidence can then help you handle other decisions in life with calm, clarity, and control.

Chapter 13: Forming Helpful Routines

Routines can give structure to your day and help you use your time more wisely. When you have a set of helpful habits, your mind does not need to wonder constantly about what to do next. Instead, you can focus on the decision-making tasks that really matter. In this chapter, we will talk about why routines are valuable, how to design them to fit your life, and how to keep them going. You will learn ways to avoid turning routines into boring chores, as well as tips on adjusting them when life changes.

1. **Why Routines Matter**

Routines are repeated actions that you do at certain times. For example, brushing your teeth when you wake up or turning off your devices before sleeping. These small actions might not seem like big decisions, but by setting them in place, you free your mind from lots of little questions every day. This can reduce stress and help you save energy for more important tasks.

When you do not have routines, you might feel scattered. Small tasks like picking clothes to wear can become time-consuming if you are always making last-minute choices. By contrast, a steady morning or evening routine helps you start or end each day calmly. Routines can also guide you toward better decisions. If exercising in the afternoon is part of your routine, you do not have to debate whether to do it—you just do it.

2. **Choosing Areas for Routines**

Not every part of life needs a strict routine. Some people like to plan every detail, while others prefer a bit more freedom. A good approach is to think about where routines would help you most. It could be:

- **Morning Routines:** Things you do right after you wake up, such as making your bed, eating a certain breakfast, or reading a few pages of a book.

- **Evening Routines:** Actions that help you wind down. These might include tidying up your space, setting clothes out for the next day, or writing down thoughts in a notebook.
- **Work or Study Routines:** Ways to handle tasks at school or on the job, like checking emails at a set time, organizing files, or writing a quick plan for the day.
- **Health Routines:** Exercise schedules, meal plans, and rest habits that keep your body and mind in good shape.
- **Family or Home Routines:** Chores, cooking times, or time spent together as a family, so everyone knows what to expect.

Pick a few areas where your day often feels rushed or disorganized. That is where a routine may help the most.

---

3. **Starting with Simple Steps**

When adding a new routine, keep it simple at first. Suppose you want a better morning pattern. Instead of listing ten tasks you must do right away, begin with one or two. For example, you could decide that right after waking up, you will make your bed and open a window for fresh air. Once you are used to that, you can add another habit, like stretching for a few minutes or writing a short note about what you want to do that day.

This approach prevents you from feeling overwhelmed. If you add too many tasks all at once, you might give up. By focusing on one small action, you can make it stick. Then you build upon that success in small steps.

---

4. **Linking New Habits to Existing Ones**

A good trick for building routines is to connect a new habit to something you already do naturally. For example, if you want to remember to drink more water, you can decide to take a glass of water right after you brush your teeth. Because you already brush your teeth at a set time, linking water to that habit makes it easier to remember.

This method, sometimes called "habit stacking," helps you rely on an existing trigger. If you always start your work by checking emails, you could attach a two-minute break to breathe or stretch right after reading your last email. Over time, the new action feels like a natural part of the existing routine.

---

5. Scheduling vs. Flexibility

Some people like to schedule each hour of the day. Others do not want that much structure. You can find a balance that suits you. Maybe you have a firm morning routine—wake up, shower, get dressed, eat breakfast, head out. But your evening can be more flexible. Or you might keep a schedule for weekdays but allow more relaxed weekends.

A schedule can lower stress by letting you predict the flow of your day. You know what you will do and when you will do it. However, too much scheduling can make you rigid. If plans change, you might get upset. Stay open to adjusting if something urgent comes up. Routines are tools to help you, not rigid rules that force you into frustration.

---

6. Adapting Routines for Different Life Stages

Routines need to change as your life changes. A routine that worked when you were a student might not fit when you start a full-time job. A routine that worked before having children might need reworking once you have a family. It is helpful to do a quick review of your routine whenever you have a big change in your life:

- **Moving to a new home**: Think about new commute times, different living spaces, or new local stores.
- **Changing jobs or schools**: Figure out your new schedule and see where a routine can save time.
- **Changes in family structure**: If you are caring for someone or have a new household member, shift chores or meal plans accordingly.

Being willing to edit your routine keeps it effective.

---

7. **Avoiding Boredom in Routines**

A routine can become dull if you never adjust it. You might start to feel you are living on autopilot, which can kill motivation. To prevent that, review your routine now and then. Ask:

- "Is this still helping me?"
- "Do I enjoy these habits?"
- "Is there a better way to do them?"

For example, if your fitness routine feels stale, maybe switch the type of exercise or change the time of day you do it. If you have always spent your evening reading in one corner, try a new reading spot or a different book genre. Small changes can refresh your routine without losing the benefits of having structure.

---

8. **Sharing Routines with Others**

If you live with friends or family, your routines might involve them too. For instance, if your household has a set dinnertime, that is a shared routine. If you want a new exercise habit with a friend, you both could decide on a time to go for a walk. Working with others can make a routine more fun and easier to keep because you keep each other accountable.

However, differences can appear. One person might prefer an early start, another might like sleeping in. If it helps to do certain tasks together, try to find middle ground. Maybe you shift the time a little so everyone can participate. Communication and compromise matter when routines affect more than just you.

---

9. **Rewards in Routines**

While a routine does not always require a reward, small positive boosts can keep you committed. For instance, if you follow your study routine for a week, you might treat yourself to a relaxing activity. If you successfully eat healthier meals for a certain period, you might enjoy a modest outing. Make sure these rewards do not cancel the progress you made. For example, if your goal is saving money, do not reward yourself by buying something expensive. Choose something simple that supports your overall aims.

Rewards can also be as small as telling yourself, "Great job!" or marking your progress on a calendar. The act of ticking off a day's habit can feel satisfying in its own way.

---

10. Handling Breakdowns in Routines

Sometimes, your routine might break. You go on a trip, get sick, or face an urgent event that disrupts your normal plan. Do not feel you have failed. Life will throw unexpected things your way. The key is to get back on track once things settle. If you cannot follow your usual routine while traveling, at least do a shorter version of it. Maybe you cannot do your full workout, but you can do a quick set of exercises or a short walk.

When you return home, take a day or two to ease back into your normal pattern. Some people try to do too much right away after a break, which can be discouraging. Instead, rebuild the habit step by step, reminding yourself that small consistency is better than no consistency.

---

11. When to Rethink or Drop a Routine

Sometimes, a routine that used to help you may no longer be useful or healthy. If you notice that a routine is causing stress or taking too much time for minimal benefits, it might be time to let it go. For instance, you may have started a daily journaling habit, but you find it no longer gives you any peace or insight. Instead, it might be adding pressure to your day.

Before dropping it, consider whether a small change could fix the problem, such as writing less each day. If that does not help, it is okay to release the habit and focus on others that feel more productive. The main point of a routine is to make life smoother, not to trap you in unnecessary tasks.

12. Automating Routines with Tools

In our modern world, many tools can help you keep routines without relying on memory. You can set alarms or reminders on your phone, use apps that track your habits, or program smart devices to do some tasks automatically. For instance, you could schedule your lights to dim at a certain hour, reminding you it is time to wind down for bed. Or you might have an app that pings you to get up and stretch every hour if you sit at a desk too long.

Used wisely, these tools can be helpful. Just be sure not to add too many or they may become distractions. Pick a few simple ones that align with your daily life. Over-relying on apps can also make you stressed by constant notifications. Aim for balance.

---

13. Connecting Routines to Long-Term Goals

Routines are not just about daily tasks; they can move you toward bigger aims. If you want to learn a new language over the next year, you can set a routine of practicing 20 minutes each day. If your goal is to write a long paper or story, you can have a routine of writing 200 words every morning. By doing these small, repeated steps, you inch closer to your bigger end result.

Seeing the link between your routine and your goal can keep you motivated. Each time you stick to your routine, you know you are one step nearer to what you want. That sense of direction makes the routine feel meaningful rather than dull.

---

14. Dealing with Lack of Motivation

Even with the best routine, you might wake up some days not wanting to follow it. Maybe you are tired, distracted, or just in a bad mood. That is normal. A routine does not fix your mood automatically, but it can help you push through times of low motivation by offering a stable path.

If you feel too discouraged, try doing just the first small step of your routine. Often, once you begin, you realize it is not as hard as you thought. If the lack of motivation lasts for a while, look deeper. Perhaps your routine needs a change, or your goals have shifted. Or maybe you need a break to recharge. The important thing is not to abandon the routine immediately—check for underlying issues first.

15. Avoiding Rigid Perfection

Some people think that once they set a routine, they must follow it perfectly every day, or else it is a failure. That thinking can lead to stress or guilt if you miss a day. Life is rarely perfect. Unexpected things happen. It is more realistic to aim for doing your routine most of the time. If you skip it for one day, you can always return to it the next day.

Allowing yourself this flexibility prevents feelings of defeat. The real power of a routine is in long-term consistency, not in being flawless. If you do something good for yourself five or six days out of seven, that is still excellent progress.

16. Routines for Different Times of Year

Seasons can affect your schedule. During certain months, school or work might be busier. In colder months, you might not want to go outside for exercise, while in warmer months, you can be more active outdoors. Think about adjusting your routine to match the season or your annual cycle. You could have a winter exercise plan that focuses on indoor workouts and a summer plan that includes walking or jogging outside.

If you have holidays or big events at certain times of the year, plan how your routine will adapt. That might include deciding in advance which habits you will pause and which you will keep doing. This planning helps you avoid feeling unprepared when the season changes.

17. Using Routines to Reduce Decision Fatigue

Decision fatigue happens when you must make too many small choices throughout the day, wearing down your focus. A routine cuts out a chunk of those small decisions. If you always know what you will eat for breakfast, you do not waste time picking among ten different foods. If you have a standard routine for getting ready for bed, you do not spend energy figuring out when to brush your teeth or what time to turn off your phone.

By putting these simple tasks on autopilot, you save mental energy for bigger decisions. This is especially helpful if your job or studies require creative thinking or problem-solving. The fewer small choices you have to puzzle over, the more mental space you have for important tasks.

---

18. Building Routines for Stress Relief

Some routines are meant not just to organize your day, but to soothe your mind. For instance, having a short breathing exercise or a minute of quiet time each morning can set a calm tone. You might do a short walk every afternoon to clear your head. You might write down three things you are thankful for before bed. These little habits can ease stress and help you stay steady when life is hectic.

By making these calming habits part of your routine, you do not have to decide when to relax—you already have a built-in moment. This can lower anxiety levels over time, because you regularly give your mind a chance to pause.

---

19. Learning from Mistakes in Routines

Not every routine you try will work well the first time. You might plan to wake up at 5 a.m. for a run, but find you are too groggy and you skip it. Or you might schedule a long reading session at night, only to realize you are usually too tired. Treat these experiences as feedback. Change the time or the way you do the task.

If you keep missing a certain habit, ask yourself why. Is it too early? Too long? Boring? Could you link it to another habit that is easier to remember? Adjusting your approach helps you create a version of the routine that fits your true lifestyle, instead of forcing something that does not match.

20. Keeping Your Routines for the Long Haul

When you find routines that truly help your life, it is worth maintaining them over time. Think about how these habits support your larger aims: maybe they boost your health, save you time, or help you learn new skills. Recognizing their value helps you stick with them when life gets busy or distractions pop up.

It can also help to track your routines once in a while. You might keep a weekly note: "Did I follow my morning routine each day?" or "How many days did I manage my planned work routine?" If you notice you have slipped, you can identify the cause and correct it quickly. Over months and years, consistent routines can lead to strong benefits, such as better well-being, improved knowledge, or more free time.

Wrapping Up Chapter 13
Forming helpful routines allows you to transform daily tasks from scattered moments into a smooth flow. By choosing areas that need structure, starting with small steps, and adjusting as needed, you can create patterns that simplify your life. Routines spare you from making countless tiny decisions and free your mind for bigger choices.

Remember to stay flexible, avoid perfectionism, and review your habits regularly. If one routine feels stale, refresh it or replace it. As you see how routines can help you achieve goals—like healthier habits, better work habits, or more peaceful mornings—you will likely want to keep refining them. Each day's small actions combine to shape bigger outcomes. With steady routines, you give yourself a reliable system that supports your decisions and reduces the everyday chaos that can derail your plans.

Chapter 14: Handling Complicated Situations

Some decisions are more than just yes or no. They involve many connected parts, uncertain outcomes, or a mix of personal, social, and practical factors. These are complicated situations where the simple methods you use for everyday choices might not be enough. This chapter looks at approaches you can use when facing more complex matters. You will learn how to organize the pieces of the problem, seek balanced facts, and remain steady even when things feel confusing.

---

1. **What Makes a Situation Complicated?**

A complicated situation often has multiple layers or parties involved. For example, deciding how to handle a serious conflict with a friend is not just about whether to stay friends or not. It might involve shared social circles, misunderstandings, past events, and future hopes. Another example could be managing a big project with many team members who have different roles or opinions.

Certain factors can make a situation complicated:

- **Large Consequences:** The outcome affects multiple areas of your life or many people.
- **Unclear Facts:** You do not have all the information you need, or facts are changing.
- **Emotional Stress:** Strong feelings might cloud your view or lead to conflicts with others.
- **Competing Values:** Different people might want different things, and it is hard to satisfy all.

When you see these signs, you know you might need a more thorough approach.

---

2. **Breaking Down the Issue**

A big decision can feel scary if you view it as one giant block. Try to break it into smaller parts so you can handle them one by one. For instance, if you are thinking about moving to another city for a new job, you might break the issue into:

- **Financial Part:** Pay, housing costs, taxes.
- **Emotional Part:** Leaving family or friends behind, feeling lonely in a new place.
- **Practical Part:** Finding a new home, arranging transport, learning about the area.
- **Career Part:** Long-term growth, new skills, network changes.

Dealing with each part separately can prevent you from getting overwhelmed. It also helps you see that some areas might be easier to address than others.

---

3. Gathering Balanced Information

In a complex matter, you usually need facts from various angles. For example, if you are negotiating a contract, you might consult an expert to understand the legal terms, check with financial advisors about your budget, and talk to people who have signed similar contracts for advice. It is easy to rely on the first source you find, but that could leave out crucial details.

Make a short list of what you need to know. For each item, think about reliable ways to find that info. Seek out more than one point of view, especially if the outcome could affect many people. A broad base of information helps you avoid big blind spots.

---

4. Mapping Stakeholders

Stakeholders are people or groups who have an interest in or can influence the situation. In a big family decision, the stakeholders might be parents, children, grandparents, and maybe even close friends. In a work project, stakeholders could be your boss, your colleagues, your clients, and maybe local regulations. Understanding who is involved helps you predict reactions and spot potential conflict.

For each stakeholder, consider:

- What do they care about?
- What resources do they control or influence?
- How might they affect the outcome if they disagree or agree?

By seeing the issue through other people's eyes, you can plan how to communicate or compromise when necessary.

---

5. **Using a Matrix or Table for Complex Choices**

For complicated decisions, a simple pros and cons list may not capture the many angles. Instead, you can create a table where you list multiple criteria along one side (like cost, time, impact on relationships, personal satisfaction) and potential choices across the top. Then, fill in how each choice ranks on each criterion. This might look like:

Criteria	**Option A**	**Option B**	**Option C**
Cost	High	Medium	Low
Time Required	3 months	1 month	2 weeks
Effect on Relationships	Harmful	Neutral	Helpful
Personal Interest Level	8/10	5/10	9/10

You can add more details in each box if needed. This table does not make the choice for you, but it shows a snapshot of each option's strengths and weaknesses. You can then decide which factors matter most.

---

6. **Staying Aware of Emotions**

Complicated decisions can stir up strong emotions like fear, anger, or excitement. Emotions are not bad—sometimes they alert you to real concerns or hidden hopes. But letting emotions run the show can lead to rash moves. If you notice you are very upset, it may help to calm down before deciding. That might mean sleeping on it, taking a walk, or talking to someone neutral.

On the other hand, ignoring your feelings might cause stress later. If something feels deeply wrong or right, ask why. Emotions can point you to deeper values or fears. Once you see the root cause, you can address it directly. Maybe you need more security, or you dislike the idea of hurting someone. Emotions can be your guide, as long as you pair them with clear thinking.

---

7. Seeking Different Perspectives

When a decision is large, talk to people who have gone through similar things. For instance, if you are deciding whether to go to college far away from home, you could chat with someone who left their hometown for school. If you are planning to start a small business, find folks who have done so. Their stories might show you pitfalls or advantages you did not see.

Remember to keep in mind that each person's experience is unique. Their path might not match yours exactly. Use what they share as insights, not as rules. Learning from others is part of handling complicated matters more wisely.

---

8. Identifying "Must-Haves" and "Nice-to-Haves"

In complicated situations, you might have a long list of wants. However, some are more critical than others. It helps to split them into two groups:

- **Must-Haves:** Non-negotiable points. If an option does not meet these, it is out. For example, you might decide you must stay within a certain budget or you must keep your children's school close.
- **Nice-to-Haves:** Desires that you prefer but can live without. For instance, having an extra bedroom might be nice but not essential, or working part-time might be a plus if everything else lines up.

Defining these groups helps you sort options faster. You focus on what truly matters first. If an option fails a must-have, you can drop it. If it meets your must-haves, you can then compare how many nice-to-haves it can offer.

---

9. Coordinating with Groups or Teams

Some complicated decisions must be made with others. This might be family members, coworkers, or friends. Team decisions can be tricky because people have different views. A practical method is to hold a meeting where you let everyone speak. Then, gather the main concerns and see where you can find agreement. If there is a conflict, you might need to negotiate.

When you coordinate with a group, clarity helps. Write down the goals you all share. Assign tasks and responsibilities so each person knows what they must do. For instance, if you are organizing an event, one person might handle the budget, another the location, another the schedule. Check in regularly to see if anyone needs help or if a problem arose. By working as a team, you can tackle bigger decisions in a more organized way.

---

10. Using Small Trials or Pilots

In some complicated situations, you can do a small test before committing fully. This is sometimes called a pilot or a trial run. For example, if you are unsure about moving to a different city, you could rent a place there for a short time or stay with a friend to feel out the area. If you want to try a new teaching method at a school, you could test it with one class for a few weeks instead of the entire school.

These tests help you gather real-world data about how the choice might work on a larger scale. If the trial goes poorly, you can adapt or decide against expanding it. If it goes well, you gain confidence and can proceed more boldly.

---

11. Planning for the Worst-Case Scenarios

With complex decisions, it is wise to imagine the worst that could happen. This is not about being negative—rather, it is about being prepared. If you decide to start a business, the worst case might be losing your investment or running into legal issues. Ask yourself: "What would I do if that happened?" or "Is there a way to lessen the impact?"

When you have a plan for the worst case, you might feel calmer. It shows you that even if things go badly, you have steps to handle it. This lowers fear and keeps you from avoiding a decision just because of scary possibilities. If the worst case seems too big, you might adjust your plan so the risk is smaller.

12. Balancing Personal Benefits and Group Needs

Some complicated decisions involve balancing what you want with the needs of others. If you are deciding whether to host a large gathering, you must think about your desire to see friends as well as their ability to attend, the cost, and any health or safety concerns. If you are leading a project at work, you might want to shine, but you also have to give your team credit and resources.

Ask yourself: "Am I only thinking about what suits me?" or "Am I giving too much weight to others and ignoring my own well-being?" A fair balance looks different in each situation, but try to see the bigger picture. Harmony often requires some give and take.

13. Recognizing When You Need Expert Help

Not all complex choices can be settled by self-reflection. If the stakes are high—like major legal or health issues—it might be best to consult an expert. A lawyer can clarify the law, a doctor can give medical advice, a financial advisor can help manage money questions. Experts have specific training or experience that you might lack.

Choosing the right expert is also important. Check their qualifications and see if they have a good reputation. It might cost money or time to seek their help, but it can prevent costly errors. If you are dealing with emotional or mental stress, a counselor or therapist might offer guidance you cannot get from friends alone.

14. Communicating Clearly with Others

In a complicated matter, misunderstandings can quickly grow. Make sure you communicate in a clear, respectful way. If there are many people involved, consider writing a summary of the situation so everyone has the same info. When discussing emotional topics, try to stay calm and use neutral language like, "I noticed this problem," rather than, "You are causing this problem."

If a conflict arises, practice active listening: let the other person speak without interruption, then repeat back what you understood. This can confirm you heard them correctly and reduce tension. Good communication often stops small problems from becoming big ones.

---

15. Knowing When to Wait

Sometimes, the wisest move in a complex situation is to wait and gather more facts, or see how events evolve. For example, if you are deciding whether to change jobs but the company might announce new positions soon, waiting a few weeks could give you better insight. If you are planning a big purchase and the market is unstable, holding off might be the smarter choice.

However, do not wait endlessly out of fear. Look for a clear reason to wait, such as a key piece of info or a scheduled event that might change your options. Once that event passes or you get the info, make a timely choice. Waiting out of avoidance can keep you stuck.

---

16. Being Ready to Adjust Plans

In complicated situations, even your best plan might need tweaking once reality hits. If you launch a product and it gets feedback that something is not working, you must decide whether to fix it or change course. If you arrange a family plan and someone's health condition changes, you must adapt.

Remaining open to new information helps you avoid doubling down on a failing choice. While it can be frustrating to shift direction, flexibility can save time and resources. Adapting quickly often prevents bigger problems later.

---

17. Managing Stress Through the Process

Complicated decisions can take a mental and emotional toll. You might lose sleep, feel anxious, or spend hours thinking about all the "what ifs." It is vital to keep yourself balanced. That might mean going for a short walk, talking to a supportive friend, or taking breaks from the problem. If you have a large project, schedule time off to recharge.

Try not to let the issue occupy every moment of your day. Simple relaxation methods—like deep breathing, stretching, or listening to calm music—can help clear your head so you think more clearly. Handling your well-being is not selfish; it is necessary to manage the complexity effectively.

---

18. Checking for Hidden Biases

We all have biases that affect how we see a complex problem. For example, you might favor a friend's idea because you like them, rather than because the idea is strong. Or you might reject an approach that reminds you of a past mistake, even if it could work now. By noticing these biases, you can push yourself to see the situation more objectively.

One way to catch biases is to ask, "If someone else had the same situation, would I give the same advice I am giving myself?" Another way is to try a little role-play: pretend you are an outside observer looking in. Ask what that observer would think. This can reveal angles you ignored before.

---

19. Making a Decision and Moving Forward

Eventually, you must act. In a complicated situation, no perfect choice might exist. You might have to pick the option that seems best with the facts you have, knowing there may be pros and cons. Once you make your decision, try to commit to it. Worrying endlessly about "what if I chose the other path?" can cause regret and second-guessing.

Of course, if you learn something major later, you can revisit your decision. But do not let fear of imperfection keep you from moving. Sometimes progress is better than waiting for a perfect answer that never appears.

20. **Reflecting on the Outcome**

After you carry out your decision and see how things turn out, take time to reflect. In complicated cases, the outcome might also be multi-layered—some parts might go well, others poorly. Look honestly at the results:

- **Did you reach the main aim?**
- **Which parts of the plan worked?**
- **Which parts would you change if you could do it again?**
- **Did any new problems appear that you did not foresee?**

These reflections are lessons for the future. Over time, each complicated situation you face can increase your skill in handling complexity. You might notice patterns in how you approach tough decisions, and you can refine your methods so you feel more prepared next time.

Wrapping Up Chapter 14
Handling complicated situations calls for more planning, broader information, and often a willingness to see other people's views. These steps can slow the process, but they help you navigate many details without drowning in confusion. By breaking the problem down, seeking balanced facts, communicating well, and being open to small tests or plan adjustments, you can keep control even when the situation has many moving parts.

It is also crucial to care for your emotional health. Complex matters can bring worry or frustration. Balancing factual analysis with emotional awareness helps you make choices that are both logical and respectful of personal or group needs. While you may never find a perfect solution to a complicated problem, thoughtful planning and readiness to adapt can lead you to an outcome you can manage and learn from. Each time you work through a complicated challenge, you add to your experience, making you more prepared for whatever else life puts in your path.

Chapter 15: Deciding When to Take Risks

Taking risks is part of life. Sometimes, a risk can lead to bigger success or new opportunities, but it can also bring the chance of failure or loss. Figuring out when to step forward and when to hold back can be tricky. This chapter explores how to size up risks, think about your comfort level, and decide if a leap is worth it. You will learn simple methods to see the upside and the downside, manage worry, and keep your eyes open for chances to grow.

Why Do We Take Risks?
People take risks for many reasons. Perhaps a person wants to reach a higher position at work or test a new idea. Sometimes, boredom with a routine can make a risky choice seem interesting. In other cases, you might take a risk to help someone you care about. There can also be social pressure if others around you are taking bold steps. Understanding why you feel pulled to take a chance helps you check if it is truly your own desire or if you are just following a crowd.

Risk itself is not bad. Without it, you might stay in the same place forever, never exploring what could be possible. However, not every risk is created equal. Some are thoughtful and based on facts, while others are random and reckless. Deciding when to take a chance is about balancing the potential benefits with the potential harm.

Recognizing Different Types of Risks
A risk can be big or small, and it can show up in different areas of life:

- **Financial Risks**: Investing in something new, changing jobs with uncertain pay, or starting a business.
- **Emotional Risks**: Telling someone how you feel, trying a public performance, or leaving a safe situation to follow a dream.
- **Physical Risks**: Doing a sport with some danger, traveling to unfamiliar places, or tackling a challenge that tests your body.
- **Social Risks**: Voicing an unpopular opinion, stepping away from a group, or joining a cause that not everyone supports.

Each type has its own potential outcomes. Knowing the kind of risk you face lets you prepare the right way. For example, you might save extra money before switching careers (financial risk), or you might practice a speech many times before delivering it to an audience (emotional risk).

Measuring Possible Gains Against Possible Losses
Before taking a risk, it helps to compare the best likely result with the worst likely result. This is a bit like making a list of upsides and downsides, but focusing on what is realistically possible. Ask yourself:

- **What do I stand to gain if this goes right?** Maybe you will learn a skill, earn money, grow your network, or find personal happiness.
- **What do I stand to lose if this goes wrong?** You might lose time, money, confidence, or even strain relationships.

By placing these two lists side by side, you get a sense of whether the upside is worth the risk of the downside. If the best outcome is very valuable—like a new career path you have always wanted—and the worst outcome is manageable, it might be worth going ahead. If the worst outcome is so damaging that you cannot recover, you might decide to rethink or adjust the plan.

Considering Your Safety Net
A safety net is something that reduces harm if the risk fails. It can take many forms:

- **Savings or Insurance**: Setting aside some money helps you bounce back from a business idea that does not succeed or from an unexpected health cost.
- **Backup Plans**: Having a second option, such as keeping part-time work while testing a new venture, can cushion failure.
- **Support System**: Friends, family, or mentors who can guide you or offer help. Their backing can lower the stress of risk.
- **Extra Skills**: If you have a wide range of skills, failing in one area will not stop you from finding another path.

A safety net does not remove the risk entirely, but it can make it less scary and more manageable. When you know you have a fallback, you may feel braver to try something new.

Starting Small to Test the Waters

Taking one giant leap can sometimes overwhelm you. If the stakes feel huge, consider trying a smaller step first:

- **Pilot Runs**: If you are thinking of launching a product, test it with a small group or on a small scale.
- **Part-Time Approach**: If you want to switch careers, see if you can do freelance or volunteer work in that field before going all-in.
- **Trial Period**: If you are thinking about moving to a new city, visit for a while or stay with a friend to sense what life would be like.

These smaller steps help you gather facts and see real outcomes. If things go well, you gain confidence. If they do not, you lose less and can still adjust or step back entirely.

Balancing Logic and Intuition

Deciding whether to take a risk is both a thinking process and a feeling process. Logic can show you the facts and numbers, but your intuition can alert you to personal values or hidden dangers that numbers alone might miss. Let's say all the data suggests a plan is sound, but you have a strong, uneasy feeling about the people involved. That gut feeling might be pointing out a real concern.

On the other hand, if your intuition strongly urges you to do something, check the facts to confirm it is not a spur-of-the-moment idea that lacks any real basis. The best choices often happen when logic and intuition agree or at least do not clash too strongly.

Identifying Your Comfort Zone

Everyone has a comfort zone, a range of actions where you feel secure. Stepping outside it can bring stress, but it can also lead to growth. The key is to know your personal limits. Some people are naturally drawn to thrilling adventures, while others prefer calmer paths. If you force yourself to take a risk that feels deeply wrong, you might face overwhelming anxiety. But if you never leave your comfort zone at all, you might miss chances to develop.

A useful approach is to expand your comfort zone bit by bit. For instance, if you want to speak in public but fear it, you could start with a small group you trust. Over time, you tackle bigger audiences. By slowly raising the level of challenge, you teach yourself you can handle more than you first thought.

Recognizing Reckless Risks

Not all risks are wise. A reckless risk might ignore obvious facts, disregard major dangers, or rely on pure hope with no evidence. For example, betting all your money on a random guess is reckless if you have not studied the odds or have no plan to deal with a bad result. Similarly, diving into a business with no research or preparation is reckless if losing that money would hurt you greatly.

A sign of a reckless risk is feeling you have no control and no knowledge. Another sign is if trusted people around you raise strong warnings based on facts, not just fear. If you still want to move forward, take a step back. Ask if you can gather more information or reduce the possible harm before jumping in.

Thinking About Timing

Sometimes, the risk itself might be okay, but the timing is off. For instance, you might want to go back to school, but your family or health situation is in a tough spot right now. That does not mean you should never return to school, just that waiting a bit might be smarter. Or maybe you have an idea for a new product, but the market is not ready. Keeping an eye on conditions can help you see if now is the best moment or if you should wait until the environment is more favorable.

There is also the risk of waiting too long and missing a window of opportunity. If a job opening you want is available now, and you are capable of doing it, waiting might let someone else take it. Balancing "not now" and "do not wait forever" is a part of risk-taking skill.

Peer Input and Mentoring

Sometimes you cannot see all sides of a potential risk on your own. Talking to a mentor, friend, or someone who has gone through a similar choice can reveal hidden points. They might warn you of a pitfall or encourage you if they see you are overthinking the dangers. Pick people who know the field or have a balanced view.

Still, remember that it is your life. Others can give you their perspective, but you decide what is best based on your goals and values. If your mentor says a risk is good but it clashes with something you deeply care about, you may want to adjust the plan or skip it.

Trusting Yourself While Acknowledging Fear
Being afraid of failure is normal. Fear can alert you to prepare better or gather more facts. At the same time, too much fear can stop you from acting even when the potential benefits are large. Trusting yourself does not mean ignoring caution. It means believing you can handle the outcome, whether good or bad. If you do fail, you can learn and try something else. If you succeed, you gain new ground.

A simple way to build self-trust is to recall past times you took smaller risks and handled the result well. Reminding yourself of those successes can reduce the fear that you will not cope with setbacks.

Setting a Limit on How Far You Will Go
Sometimes called a "stop-loss" in investing, you can set a boundary on how far you will continue taking a risk if signs turn bad. For example, if you start a business and decide, "I will invest X amount of money, and if I am still losing money after a year, I will stop or change direction." This limit keeps you from throwing too many resources into a plan that does not work.

Setting this boundary in advance also helps you think clearly when you face difficulties. Without a plan, you might stay in a failing situation out of denial or hope that things might turn around. A predefined limit can guide you to make a calmer choice.

Seeing Failure as a Step, Not an End

One reason people avoid risks is the worry about failing. Failure can feel embarrassing or costly. But many successful people had failures along the way. A failure often shows you what does not work or points out a skill you need to build. If you fail, try to see it as feedback. What went wrong? Could you have prepared differently? Which parts were out of your control, and which were in your control?

Learning from a failed risk can even open new doors. Some inventions came from accidents in the lab. Some careers took off after a person realized they needed to pivot from their original plan. Understanding that failure is a normal part of trying something new helps you stay brave enough to act.

Using Comparisons and Scenario Thinking

To gauge risk, you can compare your situation with other cases. For instance, if you want to invest in a certain market, read about people who tried it before. Did they share your background or resources? Did they succeed or face setbacks? Do not assume you will always match their outcome, but it can give you hints about what to watch for.

Scenario thinking is when you imagine different possible futures if you take a risk vs. if you do not:

- **Scenario 1**: You take the risk, and it goes well. What does life look like?
- **Scenario 2**: You take the risk, and it does not go well. What changes?
- **Scenario 3**: You do not take the risk, and life stays the same. How will you feel months or years later?

Comparing these scenarios helps you see which path you can live with. Sometimes, the regret of never trying might be worse than the regret of trying and failing.

Handling the Pressure of Risk on Relationships

If your choice affects family or friends (such as a move to a new city, or using shared finances for a project), talk with them in advance. Their support or resistance can influence both your plan and the fallout if things do not turn out well. Be honest about what you stand to lose, not just what you hope to gain. Make sure they understand your reasons. If they have valid concerns, take them seriously and see if you can adjust your plan.

At the same time, realize that no matter how much you explain, some people might still not be on board. You have to weigh their viewpoint against your own sense of purpose. If the risk is deeply important to you, perhaps you will move forward while still doing your best to limit any negative effects on your relationships.

Using Calm Decision-Making Under Pressure
Sometimes, you must decide about a risk quickly. Perhaps you get a sudden job offer that expires soon or a chance to join an exciting project on short notice. Even then, you can remain calm by focusing on the key points:

- **Check the main benefits and main dangers.**
- **See if you have a safety net or a backup plan.**
- **Listen to your gut if it is strongly uneasy or strongly enthusiastic.**
- **If possible, ask for a small extension to think.**

Rushing does not always mean you must say no. Some of life's best openings appear at unexpected times. The trick is to keep a level head while you weigh the basics of the situation.

Deciding on Gradual vs. Bold Steps
There are two broad styles of risk-taking: gradual and bold. Gradual means you take many small steps, testing each stage. Bold means you jump in more fully, trusting that you can handle what comes next. Neither style is automatically right or wrong. It depends on your personal style, the type of risk, and how quickly results must appear.

For example, if you have a short window for a life-changing chance, a bold move might be the only way. But if you have time to test and refine, a gradual approach can lower stress. Sometimes, you can combine both: start small, then jump bigger when you see positive signs.

When to Walk Away from a Risk

Sometimes, you might realize that a risk no longer makes sense. Perhaps new info shows the outcomes are worse than you first thought, or your circumstances have changed. Walking away is not always a failure. It can be a wise choice if the path you are on is leading to likely harm without enough chance of success.

If you find yourself wanting to continue out of pride or because you have already put effort in, remember that staying in a bad risk can cost more in the long run. Letting go early might let you save resources for a better opportunity. This decision can be tough if you have spent time or money, but a well-timed exit can keep you from deeper losses.

Building Your Risk Confidence Over Time

Risk-taking is like a skill. The more you do it in a thoughtful way, the more you learn. Start with smaller risks. See how you handle them. Reflect on how you felt, how you prepared, and what you might do better next time. As you gain positive experiences, you may feel more comfortable taking on bigger challenges.

If you hit a rough patch or fail, take a moment to figure out what went wrong. Did you rush? Did you skip researching? Did you ignore advice from knowledgeable people? Correcting these mistakes will sharpen your future decisions. With each risk, you gather knowledge about yourself, your environment, and your personal threshold for uncertainty.

Putting It All Together

Deciding when to take a risk involves understanding both the rewards and the dangers. You balance what you can win against what you can lose, look at your personal comfort level, and consider ways to soften the blow if things do not go as planned. You can also test ideas on a smaller scale, ask for advice, and use a calm approach even under time pressure.

Risk is not something to fear all the time. It is a tool for growth and discovery when used wisely. Sometimes it pays off with great experiences, new achievements, or personal growth. Other times, it might not go well, but you learn lessons that guide you forward. The main point is to choose your risks with thought, not throw caution to the wind. By doing so, you give yourself a chance to move beyond the ordinary and discover what you can truly do.

Chapter 16: Reviewing What Worked and What Did Not

No matter how carefully you make decisions, not everything will turn out as expected. Sometimes you reach your target smoothly, and other times you face obstacles or fail outright. When it is all done, taking time to review what went well and what did not helps you become a better decision-maker. This chapter explains how to look back in a structured way, gather key insights, and use them to sharpen your future choices. It will show you that reflection is not just about regrets; it is about finding small (and big) lessons that shape your next steps.

Why Reviewing Matters
It is tempting to move on quickly after a decision, especially if it ended poorly. But skipping a review can make you miss the lessons right in front of you. Even if a choice went well, reflecting on what helped you succeed can be just as valuable as analyzing failures. By reviewing, you see where you made wise moves, took a strong approach, or overcame an obstacle. You also see where you might have missed signs or repeated an old pattern.

Over time, these reviews can add up to a deeper understanding of how you think, how you act under stress, and what conditions enable you to perform at your best. Instead of letting each event vanish, you store the lessons so that future decisions can benefit.

Deciding When to Review
Some decisions are small, like what to eat for lunch, and might not need much reflection. Others are large—like choosing which job to take or how to handle a serious family issue—and deserve a deeper look afterward. You might also review decisions made by a group, like a team project or a family plan, to see if everyone is happy with the outcome.

A good time to review is shortly after you see results, whether good or bad. If you wait too long, you might forget details or mix them up. Still, it can help to do a second review later, once emotions calm down. That way, you can see things with fresh eyes.

A Simple Framework for Reviewing

You can use many methods to review decisions. Here is a basic outline:

- **State the Decision**: What exactly did you choose to do, and what were you aiming for?
- **Look at the Outcome**: What happened in the end? Did you meet your target, go beyond it, or fall short?
- **Identify Success Factors**: What parts of your plan worked well? Did you gather good facts, get the right help, or time things well?
- **Spot Weak Points**: Where did you struggle? Were there hidden costs, missed facts, or poor handling of stress?
- **List Possible Improvements**: If you could do it again, what would you change? Would you prepare more, set a clearer budget, or manage communication differently?

Writing these points down can turn your review into a brief record. Later, you can look at this record to remind yourself of the lessons learned.

Collecting Helpful Data

When you review, try to get facts rather than just opinions. If the decision involved money, look at actual numbers: did you spend within your plan? Did you earn what you expected? If it involved time, check how many hours you put in. If it was about learning a skill, did you pass a test or reach a certain level of ability?

Emotional or personal notes also matter. Did you feel stressed or confident during the process? Did you have conflicts with others? These details can explain why certain parts succeeded or failed. The more accurate your information, the more accurate your lessons will be.

Separating What You Controlled from What You Did Not

Sometimes, an outcome happens partly because of factors you could not control. Maybe the weather ruined an outdoor event, or a change in the economy disrupted your plan. While it is good to note these factors, do not blame them for everything. Look at the parts you did control—your planning, your spending, your communication—and see if you used them well.

By focusing on your own actions, you gain power to improve. For instance, you cannot control a rainstorm, but maybe you could have had an indoor backup plan. You cannot control a sudden shift in job demand, but perhaps you could have saved money or stayed flexible.

Dealing with Emotional Reactions
After a decision, you might feel proud, disappointed, or even upset. These feelings can color how you see the situation. To avoid letting emotions hide the truth, you can give yourself a short period to calm down before doing a serious review. If the decision ended in failure, it might hurt to look at the details right away. Take time to rest if needed, but do not ignore it forever.

If the decision ended in great success, be sure to still ask critical questions: Did you succeed because of your plan, or was luck involved? Could something have gone better? Balancing positive feelings with honest reflection can help you avoid overconfidence next time.

Learning from Others' Feedback
If other people were involved in or affected by your decision, ask for their views. They might have seen pitfalls you missed or had a different experience. For example, if you were the leader of a group project, team members might point out that the schedule was too tight or that certain tasks were unclear. Or they might say that your method of communicating worked well.

Their feedback can confirm or challenge your own conclusions. Sometimes, you might disagree with what they say. That is okay—listen with an open mind, decide what is valid, and leave the rest. Even if only part of their feedback is useful, it can still reveal areas to work on.

Recognizing Small Signs of Progress
Not every decision leads to a big, clear result. You might see smaller hints of progress. For instance, if you tried a new study method, the final grade might not have jumped right away, but you understood the material better. If you changed

your approach to healthy eating, the scale might not show a big difference yet, but you feel more energetic.

Recording these smaller gains can keep you motivated. It also helps you adjust your approach rather than discard it too soon. Sometimes, big improvements come from small, consistent changes. By spotting subtle benefits, you see that you are on a path that could pay off later.

Figuring Out Patterns in Your Decisions
Over many decisions, you might notice you always struggle in a certain area—maybe you often run out of time, or you forget to set a realistic budget, or you get into arguments with someone. These patterns can point to deeper habits or mindsets that need addressing. If you keep repeating the same issues, you can plan steps to tackle them.

Likewise, you might notice patterns in your successes. Maybe when you carefully list tasks, you finish projects faster. Or when you ask for a friend's opinion, you avoid big mistakes. These positive patterns show you what to keep doing.

Turning Lessons into Clear Tips for Yourself
It is not enough just to say, "I messed up by not managing my time." Turn that into a practical tip: "Next time, I will block out two hours each morning to work on the main task before opening my messages." If you found that talking with a teacher or mentor at the start of a project helped, make a note: "I should set a meeting early in the planning phase next time."

These tips form a personal guide you can refer to whenever a similar situation appears. Write them in a place you check often. Over time, you build a toolkit of lessons that can keep you from repeating errors or forgetting the clever approaches that worked.

Making Reviews Part of a Routine
If you only think about reviews once in a while, you might lose track of important details. Consider making a review a regular habit. For instance:

- **Weekly Review**: A quick check of smaller decisions or tasks.
- **Monthly or Quarterly Review**: A deeper look at bigger goals or projects.
- **Post-Project Review**: Right after finishing any major task or event.

During these reviews, you do not have to write a novel. A few short notes can be enough to capture the main points. By doing this regularly, you keep a clear log of your progress and do not let lessons slip away.

Staying Kind to Yourself

Reviews are meant to help you grow, not to beat yourself up. If a decision went wrong, treat it as a chance to learn, not as a sign you are doomed. Yes, you might hold yourself responsible for a mistake, but self-blame does not fix anything. Instead, focus on the question, "How can I do better next time?"

Likewise, do not get a big head if everything went right. Recognizing success is good, but remember that conditions might change in the future. See your success as a mix of solid effort, good planning, and maybe some luck. This balanced view helps you stay confident yet realistic.

Sharing Outcomes with Others

When a decision is completed, let involved people know what happened and what you learned. This could be as simple as an email summary or a short face-to-face talk. Sharing the outcome and the lessons not only helps the group learn together but also shows respect for everyone's efforts. If you were the leader, it shows you value transparency. If it was a personal decision, sharing with a close friend or family member can help them understand your growth.

Sometimes, you might get extra insights from their response: they might add details you missed, or they might see a bright side you overlooked. This exchange of ideas often leads to even deeper reflection.

Comparing Final Results to Initial Hopes

One of the easiest ways to see what worked and what did not is to compare the end result to your initial target. Ask:

- Did I do what I set out to do?
- If I fell short, how close did I get?
- Were there any unexpected positives or negatives?
- Did my view of success change during the process?

Perhaps you aimed to earn a certain amount of income with a new side project, but you earned less than expected. Yet, maybe you discovered a new skill that could pay off next time. Or you might have built a network of contacts who can help in the future. By lining up what happened with what you wanted, you see if you missed the mark or found an alternate benefit.

Using Technology to Aid Reviews
You can use apps or spreadsheets to track tasks, budgets, or progress toward goals. When the decision is done, these records provide instant data on how you performed. For example, if you used a time-tracking app, you can see exactly how many hours you put into each part of a project. Or if you used a budget app, you can see where your spending went off track.

Technology can also help you gather feedback from others through quick surveys or polls. Just be sure not to let data collection become a burden. You want enough information to guide your review without drowning in details.

Handling Group Tension in Reviews
If your project was a team effort and things went wrong, tensions can flare during the review. Some might feel they got blamed or did not receive enough help. Try to keep the discussion about the process, not personal attacks. Instead of saying, "You messed up," say, "This task was delayed—what caused the delay, and how can we avoid it next time?" Approach it as a shared problem to solve, not a person to shame.

If the group needs an outside moderator or a set of ground rules for talking, do that to keep the review calm and fair. Everyone should be able to share viewpoints without fear of harsh criticism. In the end, the goal is to figure out improvements, not to point fingers.

Watching for Hidden Success

Sometimes, you might label a decision as a failure because it did not meet the main target, yet you gained something else along the way. Maybe you built a relationship with a new mentor or learned a technique that you can use later. Or you boosted your confidence by facing a tough challenge.

If you find these hidden successes, note them as real gains. They might not have been what you planned, but they still add value to your experience. Recognizing them can ease the pain of not reaching the original goal.

Checking If Your Targets Were Realistic

A review can also show if your aim was too ambitious or not ambitious enough. If you easily crushed your target with minimal effort, maybe you could aim higher next time. If you fell short despite working very hard, maybe the target was out of reach. Adjusting your sense of what is realistic can help you set better targets in the future.

Of course, sometimes you want to aim high to push yourself. But if you repeatedly set targets far beyond what you can handle, you might end up frustrated or exhausted. A balanced target is one that challenges you yet remains within reason.

Adapting Your Methods for the Future

At the end of any review, the most important step is deciding how to use what you learned. This might mean changing your approach to time management, budgeting, or teamwork. It could also mean being more honest with yourself when setting goals. Or it might mean stepping outside your comfort zone next time if you realized you played it too safe.

Consider writing down one or two concrete actions you will take next time. For instance, "I will speak with an advisor early in the project," or "I will schedule my tasks in smaller chunks so I do not leave everything to the last minute." By noting these commitments, you give yourself a clear plan for growth.

Making Reflection Part of Your Personal Growth

Reviewing your decisions is not a one-time event. It is a mindset of continuous learning. Each time you make a choice, you gain an opportunity to grow, whether it turns out great or not. By regularly thinking about what worked and what did not, you sharpen your skills, avoid repeating mistakes, and discover paths you had not noticed before.

In time, this habit can become second nature. You will find yourself naturally asking: "What can I learn from this?" or "How can I do better next time?" That steady attitude toward improvement helps you manage the twists and turns of life with more confidence. You are no longer afraid of mistakes because you know each choice can lead to another lesson, and each lesson can move you forward.

Chapter 17: Staying Flexible and Open

Life seldom follows a simple, unchanging plan. New facts come up, fresh options appear, and unexpected events can knock you off course. In these moments, the ability to stay flexible and open can help you handle change in a calm, productive way. When you remain flexible, you are ready to shift your goals if needed, accept different ideas, and learn from things you did not expect. This chapter looks at why flexibility matters for making good decisions, how to practice being more open in day-to-day life, and ways to handle problems that come with letting go of rigid views. By the end, you will see how staying flexible can guide you to wiser choices, reduce stress, and keep you prepared for whatever comes next.

Why Flexibility Helps in Decision-Making
Flexibility in decision-making means you do not cling too tightly to a single plan or idea. Instead, you adjust when you see new facts or realize your earlier approach is not working. If you are too rigid, you might miss better routes or refuse to see signals that warn of trouble. Being open lets you spot these signs early, so you can switch paths, gather more facts, or simply pause to rethink.

Flexibility also makes you more resilient. When life throws challenges at you—a sudden job loss, a big family change, or a shift in school schedules—you can adapt more quickly. While a rigid mindset might panic or remain stuck, a flexible person asks: "How can I adjust? Where can I find help? Is there another way to reach my target?" This sense of openness means you do not see a barrier as the end of the road but as a prompt to modify your approach.

Moreover, flexibility helps you grow. Each time you adapt, you learn new skills or gather insights you can use later. You might discover you can handle tasks you never tried before or find that certain methods are surprisingly useful. By staying open, you let fresh ideas in, which can lead to better decisions in the long run.

Signs of a Rigid Mindset
To know if you need more flexibility, you can look for signs of a rigid mindset:

- **Refusing to Hear New Ideas:** If you become defensive or dismissive whenever someone suggests a change, you might be stuck in your ways.
- **Always Following One Fixed Plan:** You do not allow yourself any wiggle room, forcing yourself and others to stick to every detail, even if problems arise.
- **Fearing Any Change:** Feeling extremely uneasy about shifting your approach, even if the old way clearly fails or becomes outdated.
- **Resisting Feedback:** Rejecting or ignoring feedback because you believe you already know best.
- **Needing Perfect Certainty:** Always waiting for absolute proof or wanting every detail to stay the same before acting.

When you spot these patterns in yourself, it is a cue that some flexibility training may help. Being rigid does not mean you are "wrong"; it just means you might be limiting your potential to adapt to new truths or improved options.

Embracing a Growth Attitude
A flexible mindset often goes hand in hand with a growth attitude. This means you believe skills and insights can be expanded with work and openness. You do not see your abilities or plans as set in stone. For instance, if you fail at a new skill, a growth attitude says, "I can improve by trying new methods or putting in more practice," rather than, "I am not good at this and never will be."

To nurture this perspective, start viewing mistakes or surprises as lessons rather than setbacks. Each time an unexpected event happens, ask yourself, "What can I learn here? Is there a skill I can polish or a viewpoint I missed?" This shift in thinking paves the way for flexible decision-making because you view problems as stepping stones, not permanent blocks.

Listening to Others' Perspectives
Staying open means considering that other people's ideas might help you. This does not mean you always do what others say, but you do take the time to hear them. When you listen, you might find an angle you never thought of or a simpler route to your target. Sometimes, a friend or coworker sees details you missed because they have different experiences. By truly listening, you become more informed and can make choices that factor in a broader range of info.

Here are tips for listening well:

- **Ask Questions:** Rather than just waiting for your turn to speak, ask, "Can you explain how you reached that idea?"
- **Reflect Back:** Summarize what the other person said to make sure you got it right.
- **Stay Curious:** If you feel defensive, remind yourself you might discover something new if you hear them out fully.

By practicing these habits, you remain flexible and avoid shutting people down just because what they say conflicts with your plan.

Knowing When to Adjust Your Goals

Flexibility does not mean quitting at the first sign of trouble, but it does mean recognizing when a goal needs updating. Maybe you aimed to master a new language in six months, but you got sick or busy, so you are behind schedule. Clinging to the six-month timeline might now cause stress or sloppy work. Adjusting your goal to nine months could be more realistic. Or maybe you started a project, only to learn a more advanced method halfway through. Switching to that method, even if you lose some of your earlier efforts, might save time in the bigger picture.

Ask yourself these questions when deciding if you should adjust your goal:

- **Have new facts appeared that change the path?**
- **Is my current method causing more harm than help (like ongoing stress or weak results)?**
- **Am I ignoring signs that a different approach could be better?**

By staying flexible in your goals, you ensure that your target remains suited to your changing life, rather than trapping you in an outdated plan.

Practicing Adaptability in Daily Tasks

Being flexible is not just for big decisions. You can sharpen this skill in small, everyday ways. For example:

- **Changing Your Routine:** If you realize your morning plan no longer suits your schedule, tweak it. Maybe you do a quick task at night instead, or move your exercise to a different part of the day.
- **Trying Different Methods:** If you always study in the same spot, test a new location or technique. If you always cook the same dishes, try a simpler or faster recipe.
- **Being Open to Spontaneity:** Leave a bit of free time in your day so you can say yes to a last-minute invite or help someone out without wrecking your entire schedule.

These small actions teach your brain that change is not a threat; it can be refreshing, interesting, or more efficient. Gradually, you will find bigger adjustments less scary.

Keeping Your Core Values but Staying Flexible Elsewhere
Some people fear flexibility because they think it means giving up their beliefs or moral code. But you can keep your core values while being open about how you live them out. For example, if you value honesty, that does not change. However, you might be flexible about how you speak that honesty—sometimes a gentle approach is better than being too blunt. Or if you value kindness, you do not throw that out the window when schedules or tasks change; you just remain open about how you can show kindness in different settings.

Think of it this way: your core values are like the roots of a tree, holding it steady. Flexibility is like the branches that sway in the wind. The trunk and roots do not vanish, but the branches bend so they do not snap in a storm. In the same way, you do not have to drop your convictions, but you can let small habits or methods shift to handle changes in your environment.

Staying Flexible Without Being Indecisive
One worry about flexibility is that you might never make up your mind because you are always open to yet another viewpoint. There is a difference between being flexible and being indecisive. Flexibility means you pick a path after considering the facts, but you remain ready to shift if you see strong reasons to do so. Indecision means you never commit to a path at all, getting stuck in endless loops of "what if" scenarios.

A healthy approach is to give yourself a deadline. Gather enough facts, weigh your options, then decide. Stay alert to signs that you need to pivot later, but do not keep waiting for the perfect moment or perfect data that may never come. This way, you blend decisiveness with openness.

Learning from Changing Circumstances

Sometimes, outside events force you to be flexible. A job might relocate you, a sudden policy might change your school or workplace rules, or a personal situation might shift. When such things happen, you can either dig in your heels and deny reality or quickly learn what these changes mean and adapt. The second option is usually less stressful in the long run. While the first reaction might be anger or confusion, try to move past that stage to acceptance and practical steps.

For example, if your workplace suddenly adopts new software, do not spend all your energy complaining. Instead, see how you can learn it quickly, ask for help from someone who catches on faster, and figure out if this tool might help you do your tasks better. By doing so, you remain open to the positive side of a forced change.

Staying Open to Unusual Solutions

Sometimes the best answer to a problem is not the typical one. Flexible thinkers allow for odd or creative ideas. Suppose your team is stuck on a tough project. A rigid approach might say, "We must do it the standard way." But an open approach might invite brainstorming sessions where every idea is listed, even the ones that sound strange at first. Out of that session, a unique solution could emerge.

It is not about picking every wild idea, but about letting them be heard and weighed. Being open means allowing space for ideas you initially think are odd. This readiness can lead you to discover an approach that everyone else missed because they were sticking to what is normal or comfortable.

Handling Anxiety About Uncertainty

Flexibility can be stressful if you dislike the unknown. Letting go of a firm plan sometimes means you do not know what will happen next. If you find yourself anxious, try these strategies:

- **Focus on What You Can Control:** You might not control the overall outcome, but you can decide how much you prepare or how you manage your day-to-day tasks.
- **Break Tasks Down:** If the path ahead is unclear, take small steps. Even a bit of progress can reduce anxiety about the bigger picture.
- **Remind Yourself of Past Adaptations:** Think back to times you handled changes well. If you did it before, you can probably do it again.
- **Speak with Supportive People:** Sharing your concerns helps you see that others face uncertainty too and can offer guidance on staying open without panic.

Over time, you might grow more comfortable with the idea that some things cannot be fully predicted.

Building a Habit of Reflection

Being flexible does not mean you blindly jump from one idea to another. You can support your openness by regularly reflecting on how things are going. For instance, at the end of each week, take a few minutes to think:

- **What changed this week, and how did I respond?**
- **Did I miss an opportunity to adjust when I should have?**
- **Did I switch plans too soon without giving them a fair try?**

This short reflection can show you patterns. Maybe you realize you resist change in a certain type of situation or that you pivot too quickly in another area. By spotting these habits, you can fine-tune your approach to flexibility, becoming neither too stiff nor too quick to abandon a decent plan.

Allowing Others to Influence You

Flexibility includes letting yourself be influenced by others' good ideas. If a friend shows you a better way to solve a math problem, you can adopt it rather than clinging to your old method just because it is familiar. Or if a coworker explains a new process that saves time, try it out. Being influenced does not mean you have no personal stance; it means you are wise enough to admit that others sometimes know a more efficient approach.

Some people avoid letting others influence them because they want to appear independent or in control. But true independence often includes the ability to learn from those around you. In the end, you make the final choice of whether to incorporate their idea or not.

Maintaining Focus While Staying Open
You might worry that being open to new ideas will scatter your attention too much. The key is to keep track of your main goals or values. Let's say your main goal is to improve your skills as a musician. Being open means you might try different practice routines, different songs, or new instruments. However, you still remain focused on getting better at music overall. You do not suddenly throw away your aim and dive into something that has no connection to your musical improvement.

Setting a guiding question can help. For music, that question might be, "Does this new idea or tool help me grow as a musician?" If yes, you explore it; if no, you skip it. This method ensures you stay flexible without losing your direction.

Being Flexible When Working with Groups
In group decisions, flexibility is extra valuable. Different people bring different perspectives, and a rigid approach might shut them down. If you lead a group project, you can say, "Here is our main goal, but how we get there can be decided together." That way, people feel more involved. They might have insights you never expected. If your original plan is outvoted by a strong argument for a new idea, being flexible means you let the group try it. If it fails, you can revisit your initial plan or develop another approach.

This group-based flexibility often builds trust, too. Team members see that their input matters. They might return the favor by being open to your guidance when you need them to follow a certain structure. Flexibility in a group context fosters shared ownership of decisions, reducing conflicts that arise when one person insists on controlling every detail.

Letting Go of the Fear of "Wasted Effort"

One reason people avoid changing plans is the feeling that the work they already did will be "wasted." But sticking to a failing route just because you invested time in it can lead to bigger losses. A flexible person sees those past efforts as part of learning, not a waste. For instance, if you spent a month studying a topic and realize a different approach suits you better, the knowledge gained is still useful in some way. Maybe it gave you background context or sharpened your ability to research.

Instead of viewing adjustments as tossing away what you already did, think of them as redirecting your efforts toward a more promising outcome. That viewpoint removes the guilt or regret that sometimes blocks people from moving forward.

Balancing Tradition with Fresh Thinking

Some tasks or traditions have been around for a long time. People do them a certain way out of habit or respect for history. While traditions can have value, a flexible mindset asks if the tradition still fits present needs. If it does, great—keep it. If it does not, maybe it is time to tweak it or replace it. This does not mean disrespecting the past but recognizing that the world evolves.

For example, a company might hold certain meetings every week because they always have. However, if employees feel these meetings no longer serve a purpose, a flexible leader might change the format or frequency. People can say, "We appreciate the reason these meetings started, but how can we update them for today's demands?"

Teaching Flexibility to Younger People

Parents, teachers, or mentors can help kids learn flexibility by showing them how to adapt. For instance, if a child wants to build a model and the instructions are unclear, encourage them to try different building methods. Let them see that it is okay to switch pieces around, experiment, and learn from mistakes. Praise their willingness to try again rather than shaming them for not following the plan.

When younger people see adults handle changes calmly, they learn that unexpected events do not need to be scary or upsetting. Instead, they become moments to explore new solutions. This skill prepares them for real-world challenges that rarely go exactly as planned.

Examples of Flexibility in Real Life

- **Job Shifts:** A person trained as an accountant but realized mid-career they enjoy helping people face-to-face. They switch into a related field, maybe financial counseling, adapting their existing skills (money management, attention to detail) to a new context.
- **Academic Adjustments:** A student sets out to major in biology but discovers an interest in data science. They remain open to combining both, possibly going into bioinformatics.
- **Personal Goals:** Someone aims to learn painting, but after trying different art forms, they find they prefer sculpture. They change direction without feeling it was a waste to practice painting, because it taught them basic art concepts.
- **Community Projects:** A group wants to build a playground. After hearing neighbors' ideas, they modify the original design to include a space for community gatherings.

In each case, the person or group started with one vision but stayed open to shifting based on new insights or changing desires. The result was often more satisfying or effective.

Making Flexibility Part of Your Personal Growth

Staying flexible is an ongoing practice, not a one-time task. Each situation that challenges your original view is a chance to expand your openness. Sometimes you will find that staying on your chosen path is still correct after re-checking. Other times you will pivot. Either way, the key is that you are willing to adapt rather than default to a single viewpoint just because you started with it.

You can:

- **Schedule Periodic Check-Ins:** Once a month or once a quarter, ask yourself if your goals, methods, or routines need adjustment.
- **Seek Variety:** Read or watch sources outside your usual comfort zone to expose your mind to fresh perspectives.
- **Practice Calm Under Stress:** If an unexpected change happens, pause and breathe before reacting. Remind yourself that some flexibility might be needed.
- **Celebrate Small Shifts:** Notice when you adapt in a small way and see that it benefited you, like trying a new route to work and finding it saves time.

By making flexibility and openness part of your overall approach to life, you will likely feel less anxiety about the unknown. You will see that change can be an ally, not an enemy. And as you gather more experience in adjusting gracefully, you will find decision-making becomes smoother: you gather info, decide on a path, stay watchful for signs to shift, and remain at ease if shifting is necessary.

Wrapping Up Chapter 17

Staying flexible and open means recognizing that plans may shift, new facts may appear, and other people's insights can improve your ideas. It does not imply you have no direction; rather, it means you keep a strong sense of your main values or goals while letting the details vary as needed. This approach reduces panic when things deviate from the script. It also helps you spot breakthroughs you might have overlooked if you clung to a single viewpoint. By embracing this mindset in small daily ways and larger decisions, you equip yourself to handle life's twists and turns with calm, curiosity, and a readiness to adapt.

Above all, remember that being flexible does not mean being weak or uncertain. It means you are wise enough to realize that sticking to an approach that no longer works can be more harmful than trying something different. In the next chapter, we will look at facing doubts and uncertainty directly. There, you will see how an open mind and a willingness to adapt can be strong tools when you are not sure about which path is right for you. Flexibility is the bridge that turns worry about the unknown into a constructive search for clearer insight.

Chapter 18: Facing Doubts and Uncertainty

No matter how carefully you plan or how much research you do, doubt and uncertainty can creep in when you have to choose a path. Sometimes, the stakes are high—you might be deciding on a career move, a big purchase, or a relationship step—and you are not certain you have the best information or that your choice will lead to the outcome you want. Doubt and uncertainty can feel uncomfortable, even scary. Yet they are a normal part of making decisions in a world where no one has a crystal ball. This chapter explores why doubts happen, how to handle uneasy feelings about the unknown, and ways to move forward even when you do not have every answer. By the end, you will see that uncertainty does not have to paralyze you. Instead, it can be a signal to think carefully, stay open to new facts, and trust your ability to handle the results.

Why Doubts Appear
Doubts arise for several reasons:

- **Fear of Failure:** You might worry you will choose wrongly and mess everything up, leading to regrets or judgments from others.
- **Overthinking:** You might gather so many details that you start questioning every tiny factor, unsure which ones really matter.
- **Pressure to Be Perfect:** If you set very high standards for yourself, any uncertainty can feel like a risk of not meeting those standards.
- **Past Mistakes:** Maybe you made a poor decision before, so you doubt your ability to choose well now.
- **Lack of Experience:** When trying something totally new, you naturally feel unsure because you have no track record to guide you.

These causes are normal. Everyone experiences a mix of them at different points. Recognizing the root of your doubts can help you handle them more calmly. For instance, if fear of failure is the main driver, you can focus on preparing a backup plan so you are less worried about a worst-case scenario.

Uncertainty vs. Doubt
Uncertainty means you do not know the future or all the facts. Doubt is an

emotional response to that uncertainty, a feeling that says, "I am not sure if I am making the right choice." You can be uncertain without much doubt if you are confident you can adapt no matter what. But if you lack confidence or see high risks, you might have strong doubts.

Understanding this difference can guide your response. If your main issue is uncertainty (lack of facts), you can gather more info, ask experts, or run small tests. If your main issue is doubt (fear you cannot handle it), you might work on building self-confidence, seeking moral support, or facing your fear of mistakes.

Accepting That Some Level of Uncertainty Is Normal
No human can predict everything. Economic trends, personal relationships, technology changes—many parts of life can shift with little warning. Trying to remove all uncertainty is often impossible. If you demand 100% clarity before acting, you might never make a move. Instead, aim for a "good enough" view of the situation. That might be 70–80% clarity, leaving room for the unknown. Once you reach that level, consider making a decision and trusting you can adapt if surprises happen.

Give yourself permission to not know everything. A lot of stress comes from thinking you must be all-knowing or always "right." Real-life decisions often involve partial facts and guesswork, so acknowledging that from the start can relieve pressure.

Breaking the Illusion of a Perfect Choice
People sometimes doubt themselves because they imagine there is a perfect choice out there, and they worry about missing it. In truth, many decisions have multiple "good enough" options, each with pros and cons. Focusing on finding the single best choice can fuel endless doubt. Accepting that more than one path might work frees you to pick an option that feels solid without overthinking whether there is a "perfect" alternative.

It helps to remind yourself that the perfect choice, if it exists at all, might only become clear in hindsight. You cannot judge a path you did not take, and often the differences are subtle. Let go of the quest for perfection and aim for a choice that aligns with your values, resources, and current insights.

Managing Information Overload

An overload of facts can feed uncertainty. You might read many articles, consult too many people, or watch an endless stream of videos on a topic. While it is good to be informed, there is a point where extra input no longer helps—it just overwhelms you. If you feel stuck, ask yourself if you already have the main points needed to decide.

One method is to set a clear limit. For example, promise yourself you will read only three credible sources or talk to only two experts before deciding. Once you hit that limit, stop gathering data and shift to sorting it out. This approach keeps you from being trapped in a cycle of continuous research that never ends.

Using Small Experiments to Test the Waters

Doubts often come from not knowing how something will play out. Doing a small experiment, if possible, can give you a peek at what to expect. For instance, if you are unsure about living in a new city, visit there for a weekend or stay with a friend. If you want to switch to a new career, take on a small side project in that field. These short tests might not remove all doubts, but they give real-life data that can lower your uncertainty.

If the test goes well, you gain confidence. If it does not, you can adjust your plan or decide it is not the right path. Either way, you move forward with more clarity, rather than staying frozen in "what if" thoughts.

Dealing with the Fear of Regret

Doubt often links to regret: "What if I make this choice and regret it later?" But regret can happen even if you do nothing. If you pass on an opportunity, you might regret not trying. Ask which regret seems easier to handle: the regret of failing or the regret of never finding out?

It can help to reframe regret as a lesson. If you choose a path and it does not go well, you might regret some outcomes, but you also learn something. That knowledge can guide your next choice. Meanwhile, not choosing at all can leave you with no new insights. Seeing regret in this light eases the fear, because even a misstep can have a silver lining if you look for the lesson.

Talking Through Your Doubts

Sometimes, speaking your doubts aloud to a friend, family member, or mentor clarifies them. They might ask questions that highlight gaps in your thinking or remind you of strengths you forgot. Or they might share a story of how they faced similar worries. Even if they do not provide a direct answer, the act of expressing your doubts can help you see them more objectively.

Pick someone who will listen without judgment, and who can offer honest feedback. It is not about letting them decide for you; it is about getting a second viewpoint or simply releasing the tension that builds when you keep doubts bottled up.

Crafting a Backup Plan

One way to manage uncertainty is to prepare a backup plan in case your main choice fails. For example, if you are starting a small business, keep an option to return to part-time work or consult in your old field. If you decide to move to a new city, set aside enough savings so you can relocate back if it truly does not work out. Knowing you have a safety net can lower your sense of risk and allow you to move forward despite doubts.

A backup plan should be realistic. If your plan depends on winning the lottery or on someone giving you a huge gift, that may not truly reduce your worry. Instead, find a simpler route that you could realistically follow if needed, so you feel less cornered by fear of failure.

Facing the "Worst Case" Head-On

Sometimes, doubts loom because we avoid looking at the worst-case scenario in detail. We fear it might be too terrible to even consider. Yet when you actually spell out what the worst case looks like, you often see it is something you might recover from. For instance, if the worst case is losing some money or facing embarrassment, you might realize you could still bounce back.

Try an exercise: Write down the worst outcome of your decision. Then list how you would handle it if it occurred. Would you get another job? Ask for help from someone? Downsize for a while? This process makes the worst case less mysterious. You might see it is not as impossible as your imagination suggested.

Knowing That Doubts Can Protect You

Doubts are not always a bad thing. Sometimes they warn you about real dangers. For example, if you have a gut feeling that a certain business partner is not reliable, that doubt could be a sign to investigate further before signing anything. If you doubt your readiness for a big race you have not trained enough for, maybe that is your body's way of signaling you to prepare more.

The key is to listen to your doubts without letting them run your entire decision process. Ask, "Is there actual evidence behind this concern, or is it just fear?" If the evidence is valid, use it to adjust your plan or do more preparation. If the doubt stems from old anxiety or a vague worry, you might keep it in mind but move forward with caution.

Building Tolerance for the Unknown

In many chapters, we discussed tools like self-awareness, emotion management, and adaptability. These tools help you face the unknown without crumbling. Tolerating uncertainty is like building a muscle: the more often you deal with uncertain situations and see that you can handle them, the less power doubt has over you.

You can start small. Put yourself in minor uncertain situations: try a new dish without knowing if you will like it, or join a small group activity you have never done before. Each time you survive one of these moments, remind yourself, "I did something uncertain, and I handled it." Over time, bigger uncertainties become less frightening.

Practicing Mindfulness to Ease Doubt

Doubt often comes with racing thoughts and what-if scenarios flooding your mind. Mindfulness techniques—like focusing on your breath or doing a short body scan—can slow these racing thoughts. By paying attention to your present moment, you give your mind a rest from spinning about the future. Once calmer, you can review your decision more rationally.

A basic mindfulness exercise could be closing your eyes, breathing in for a count of four, holding for a second, then exhaling for a count of four. Do this several times, noticing how your chest and stomach move. This small pause breaks the loop of worry thoughts, letting you come back to the choice with less anxiety.

Finding Confidence in Past Successes

If you doubt your ability to make a good choice, look back at times you handled decisions well—even small ones. Maybe you chose a study method that boosted your grades or picked a volunteer role that taught you valuable lessons. Recall how you made that choice and how you dealt with challenges. This reminder can reduce doubt by showing you have some history of success.

Even if you have faced mistakes or failures, you likely also have moments when things turned out well because of your efforts. Gathering these memories offers proof you are not entirely clueless. You have navigated uncertainty before, so you can do it again.

Setting a Decision Deadline

When doubts linger too long, they can lead to decision paralysis. One technique is to give yourself a firm deadline: "I will decide on this by Friday," or "Once I finish reading these three documents, I will pick an option." That way, you do not let doubts stretch on indefinitely. You still allow time for thought and research, but you limit it, forcing yourself to move from the thinking phase to the acting phase.

If the decision is big, the deadline can be a few weeks or months away, but it should still be specific. Mark it on a calendar. As the date nears, start finalizing your thoughts. This method keeps doubt from growing without end.

Turning Doubt into Action

If you find yourself repeatedly thinking, "I am not sure if this will work," translate that doubt into a question: "What can I do to increase the chance of success or to confirm if it will work?" This might mean testing a small piece of the plan, speaking to someone who has done it before, or setting up a safeguard. By turning doubt into a specific action, you move from worry to problem-solving.

For example, if you doubt you can afford a certain life change, you might sit down and do a thorough budget calculation or talk to a financial advisor. If you doubt you can handle a demanding schedule, do a trial week where you live by that schedule to see how it feels. Each step you take reduces the unknown.

Accepting the Possibility of Being Wrong

No one likes being wrong, but it happens. Sometimes, you gather facts, weigh them, and still end up with an outcome that is not what you hoped. Facing doubt means accepting you might be mistaken. But that acceptance can be freeing—you realize that being wrong does not mark the end of your story. You can try again, revise your method, or look for new opportunities.

People who fear being wrong might avoid decisions altogether, leading to missed chances. By embracing the idea that mistakes are part of learning, you break free from that fear. This view helps you take action even amid uncertainty because you trust in your own resilience.

Asking for Small Confirmations Along the Way

When a decision spans weeks or months, you do not have to wait until the end to see if you are on the right track. Set up checkpoints. For example, if you are launching a creative project, you might show a rough draft to a mentor or friend to gather thoughts early. If you are changing your exercise habits, track your progress every two weeks. These small confirmations either reassure you that you are doing fine or reveal issues before they become huge problems.

This approach can greatly reduce doubt because you are not flying blind. You collect feedback in stages and can pivot if you see warning signs. It also boosts your confidence when the feedback is positive, making you less prone to second-guess yourself.

Keeping a Record of Your Decision Process
Writing down your thinking process can help you manage doubts. List the pros, cons, facts, and opinions you have considered. Note what you decided and why. If doubts arise later, you can revisit your notes. You might see you made a rational choice based on the info you had. Or you might spot an area you overlooked, which you can address.

This record serves as a reference point to remind you that you did not pick randomly—you took logical steps. It can also guide you if you ever face a similar decision in the future. By seeing how your logic played out, you refine your approach for next time.

Moving Forward Despite Uncertainty
Ultimately, there comes a moment when you must choose, doubts or not. The perfect clarity you crave may not appear. By using the strategies outlined—gathering enough information (not too much), making small tests, leaning on your support network, and calming your fear of mistakes—you give yourself a solid footing even if the ground feels shaky.

The important thing is to act. Standing still because you are uncertain can sometimes be the worst outcome, leading to missed growth and lingering regret. By deciding, you either succeed, learn a lesson, or both. In a sense, that is a victory no matter which direction events take. Doubt becomes manageable once you accept that uncertainty is part of any bold move, and that your inner strength and resources allow you to handle what follows.

Closing Thoughts on Chapter 18
Facing doubts and uncertainty is not about waiting for the day when you feel 100% sure—because that day might never come. Rather, it is about realizing that most big steps involve incomplete facts and that your feelings of doubt can be a healthy sign you are taking a choice seriously. By shaping your doubt into thoughtful preparation, seeking help, and practicing acceptance of potential mistakes, you harness uncertainty as a tool rather than a roadblock.

Chapter 19: Keeping Up Motivation

Motivation is the fuel that helps you continue working toward your targets, even when things get tough. Some days, you feel inspired and ready to tackle challenges with excitement. Other times, you might feel drained, unsure, or bored. Learning how to keep up your motivation can make a big difference in how you progress with decisions and actions. This chapter explores what motivation is, why it rises and falls, and what you can do to boost it when it gets low. You will see how simple habits and mindset shifts can keep you going, especially when tasks or goals take a while to reach.

Why Motivation Matters
Motivation pushes you to stay on track with your plans instead of quitting at the first obstacle. It gives you the energy to tackle daily tasks, prepare for the future, and handle issues that pop up. Without it, even simple activities can feel like a burden. You might delay tasks, lose interest in your aims, or feel hopeless about making progress. On the other hand, a healthy level of motivation makes it easier to see the value in what you are doing and to keep going, even if results are not instant.

When you understand the role of motivation, you can spot why you sometimes feel excited and other times do not. This awareness helps you create an environment—both mental and physical—that supports steady progress rather than constant ups and downs.

The Two Main Types of Motivation
Psychologists often talk about two kinds of motivation:

- **Internal (Intrinsic) Motivation**: This comes from within you. You work on something because you genuinely like it, find it interesting, or see it as personally meaningful. For example, an artist might paint simply because they love the process of creating images.
- **External (Extrinsic) Motivation**: This is driven by outside rewards or pressures. You do it for a paycheck, to avoid punishment, or for a prize.

For instance, you might study hard to get top grades because your parents expect it, or because you want a scholarship.

Each type has its place. External motivation can get you started when tasks are not thrilling on their own, like cleaning your room to avoid trouble or finishing a work project because you need the income. However, internal motivation tends to produce deeper satisfaction and longer-lasting effort. If you connect your tasks to personal values or enjoyment, you often keep going even without a big reward or threat.

Finding Your "Why"
To sustain motivation, it helps to know why you want to achieve a particular aim. For example, if you want to learn a second language, ask why. Is it to travel with more ease, talk to relatives who speak that language, or expand your job options? If your main reason is truly personal, you are more likely to stay motivated than if you are only doing it because someone else said you should.

Try writing down a simple statement of your "why." For instance: "I want to learn this skill because it will let me help people in my community." Or "I am saving money so I can start my own business next year." Placing this statement somewhere visible—on a note by your desk, in your phone's reminders—can remind you daily of the deeper purpose behind your actions.

Setting Clear and Achievable Targets
Motivation often fades when your aims feel too vague or too large to handle. That is why chapters on defining targets and forming routines stress being specific. If you break a huge goal into smaller steps, you can see real progress. Each time you complete a step, you gain a sense of achievement that fuels you to tackle the next one.

When you notice your motivation dropping, look at your targets. Are they still realistic? Are they too big and making you feel overwhelmed? Adjusting them to a more doable size can restore your drive. If you aim to write a book, for example, set a weekly word count. Knowing you only have to produce a certain number of words each day can feel more manageable than thinking about completing 200 or 300 pages all at once.

Using Small Rewards and Positive Feedback

While internal motivation is powerful, giving yourself small rewards along the way can keep your spirits up, especially during dull or repetitive tasks. A reward does not have to be expensive or fancy. It might be taking a short break, enjoying a snack you like, or giving yourself free time to do an activity you find fun. After finishing a milestone, you can say to yourself, "Well done, I have earned 15 minutes of reading a favorite comic," or "I will watch an episode of a show I enjoy."

Positive feedback also matters. Even a small internal message like, "I did well on that assignment; I am proud of my effort," can boost motivation. If you have friends or family who support you, share your little successes with them. Hearing "Good job" from someone who cares can help you keep going.

Tracking Progress Visually

People often stay more motivated if they can see how far they have come. You might keep a chart, checklist, or calendar where you mark each step you finish. For instance, if you are training for a sports event, you can note how many miles you ran or how many times you practiced each week. If you are saving money, you might color in a progress bar each time you put some amount into your savings.

Visually seeing your efforts add up—even if it is just a few boxes or lines—reminds you that you are not standing still. This helps fight the feeling that you are not getting anywhere. It also stirs up positive feelings as your progress lines or checkmarks build over time.

Dealing with Setbacks

Motivation can plunge when you face a setback, like a failed test, an injury that stops your training, or a financial shortfall. At times like these, it is easy to feel like giving up. Yet setbacks are often temporary or can be worked around. Ask yourself: "Is there another route to the same aim? Do I need more time or a different strategy?" By reframing setbacks as signals that you need to adjust, you keep motivation from collapsing.

It also helps to remember times when you overcame a setback before. Perhaps you faced difficulty in a past project and still found a way forward. Let these memories remind you that bouncing back is possible. If the setback seems huge, break your recovery steps into small tasks to avoid feeling overloaded.

Keeping Energy Levels Up
Physical tiredness and stress can drain motivation. If you are always exhausted, even an exciting goal can feel like too much work. That is why caring for your basic needs is part of staying motivated:

- **Get Enough Rest**: Lack of sleep makes concentration and drive harder to maintain.
- **Eat Balanced Meals**: Heavy junk food can make you feel sluggish, reducing your push to get things done.
- **Stay Active**: Light exercise, even a brief walk, can boost mood and clarity.
- **Manage Stress**: Quick tension relievers—like deep breathing or short breaks—keep you from feeling overwhelmed by daily worries.

When your body and mind have enough energy, motivation finds firmer ground to stand on.

Surrounding Yourself with Encouraging People
The people around you can affect your drive. If your friends or coworkers are always negative or do not believe in self-improvement, you may find it tougher to stay motivated. Try connecting with those who share your goals or who at least support them. This might mean joining a study group, a sports club, an online forum, or spending more time with friends who encourage you.

Hearing about others' progress can also spark your own motivation. If you see a classmate or neighbor achieving a similar target, you might think, "If they can do it, I can too." Motivation can be contagious when you interact with people on a similar path or who share a positive mindset.

Varying Your Approach for Long Projects
If a goal will take months or years—like getting a degree or mastering an art form—motivation can dip because the end seems far away. One strategy is to add variety to your daily or weekly routine so you do not get stuck in a dull grind. If your method has been the same for a long time, try changing it up:

- **Alternate Task Orders**: If you always tackle tasks in one order, mix them up. For instance, if you study reading first and math second, switch them around to keep your mind alert.
- **Learn New Techniques**: If you are learning piano and are bored with the same drills, look into a different style of music or practice approach.
- **Add Challenges**: Sometimes, you lose motivation because a task has become too easy. Setting a slightly higher challenge can reignite interest.

Keeping things fresh helps you stay mentally engaged and prevents boredom from undermining your energy.

Breaking Down the "All or Nothing" Thought
Some people lose motivation if they do not meet every small milestone perfectly. If you miss one gym session or fail one quiz, you might think, "Everything is ruined," and give up entirely. This "all or nothing" view is harmful because a single misstep does not erase all your past progress. A more balanced approach is: "I made a mistake or missed a day, but I can still continue." By accepting small slips, you keep your overall plan intact rather than discarding it at the first sign of imperfection.

Recognizing Small Wins
When you are working toward a bigger success, do not wait until the very end to see any positive results. Notice and appreciate small improvements. If you are trying to improve your writing, and you manage to write a paragraph more smoothly today than yesterday, that is progress worth noting. If you are trying to learn a new software, and you finally grasped a tricky shortcut, give yourself a small nod of recognition.

These small wins might look insignificant, but they add up and sustain a sense of momentum. Each little accomplishment can serve as a reminder that you are moving forward, which keeps your flame of motivation alive.

Connecting Tasks to Personal Enjoyment
If a task seems boring, try to pair it with something you find pleasurable, as long as it does not distract you. For example, you could put on your favorite calm music while cleaning or plan your study sessions at a cozy café so the environment feels pleasant. You might also turn some tasks into mini-games or challenges. If you have a pile of paperwork, you could time yourself to see how efficiently you can sort it while keeping accuracy.

This approach transforms otherwise dull tasks into something a bit more engaging. However, be mindful not to overshadow the task with the fun element. The idea is to make the chore more bearable, not to lose focus on what needs to be done.

Reviewing and Renewing Goals Periodically
Motivation can fade if your aim or situation has changed but you keep pushing an old plan. Schedule a brief check every few weeks or months to confirm if your target still fits your life. If it does, reaffirm why it matters. If it no longer matches your values or resources, adjust it. Sticking blindly to a goal that no longer serves you can drain motivation because part of you senses it is no longer right.

Even if the target remains the same, reviewing it can recharge your enthusiasm. Remind yourself of your main reasons and see how much progress you have made so far. This reflection can light the spark again if you have been running on autopilot.

Embracing Self-Compassion
Harsh self-criticism can crush motivation. If every time you slip you call yourself names or declare you are worthless, you create a hostile internal environment. Instead, practice a kinder outlook: treat yourself as you would treat a close friend who is struggling. You might think, "I had a setback, but it is okay. I will try

again." This does not mean ignoring mistakes; it means not beating yourself up for them. Self-compassion helps you stay calm and keep your desire to improve, rather than destroying your will with negative self-talk.

Motivating Yourself by Visualizing Outcomes

Sometimes, picturing the results of your effort can keep you inspired. If you dream of finishing a course, imagine yourself holding the certificate or using the knowledge in a real job. If you want to learn a musical instrument, picture playing a tune in front of a small group of friends who are proud of you. If you seek better health, imagine having more stamina for daily tasks.

Visualization can be a brief mental exercise. Close your eyes for a minute, see yourself enjoying the fruits of your labor, and feel the positive emotion that comes with it. This mental boost can refresh your drive, especially on days when the grind feels tough.

Managing Peer or Social Media Comparisons

A motivation killer can be comparing yourself to others who seem to reach the finish line faster or with less effort. Social media often shows people's highlights without the struggles behind the scenes. If you let these comparisons bother you, you may lose faith in your progress. Remember, each person's situation is different—different starting points, backgrounds, and resources.

Focus on your own path. Measure your progress against your past self, not against someone else's story. If you do see a friend achieving something that you want, let it be an example that it can be done, rather than proof you are behind. Switching that mindset can keep your motivation from being drowned by envy or pressure to measure up.

Knowing When to Take Breaks

Sometimes, pushing too hard for too long can lead to burnout, a state of deep exhaustion that kills all motivation. If you sense you are hitting a wall—feeling constant tiredness, lack of excitement, or resentment about your tasks—step back for a bit. This could mean a short vacation, a weekend off, or even a single day where you do not follow your usual schedule.

The key is to rest responsibly. Do not run away from your aim entirely; just grant yourself enough pause to recharge. When you return, you might find your enthusiasm renewed because your mind and body had time to recover.

Asking for Support or Mentorship

If your motivation stays low for a long stretch, consider seeking guidance from a counselor, coach, or mentor. These professionals or experienced individuals can help you uncover the mental blocks holding you back. They might suggest new strategies for time management, stress handling, or emotional balance. Sometimes, just talking through your goals and difficulties with an understanding mentor can spark new motivation you did not realize you had.

Additionally, if your motivation is linked to deeper issues—like anxiety, sadness, or major life stress—a mental health professional can offer targeted support. Motivation is not just a personal matter; outside help can be the key to getting back on your feet if things feel overwhelming.

Moving Forward with Renewed Drive

Motivation naturally ebbs and flows, but you have many tools to keep it from crashing completely. By clarifying your "why," setting realistic steps, rewarding yourself, managing stress, and staying in contact with encouraging people, you create a foundation that supports motivation over the long haul. Each time you sense your drive slipping, take a moment to check the basics: Are you tired? Are your targets too large or too vague? Are you forgetting your deeper purpose?

You do not have to feel excited every day. Even a steady, moderate level of motivation can keep you moving. On days when you feel especially fired up, make use of that energy to leap forward. On days when you feel less so, rely on structure and supportive habits to get through. Over time, you will see that a combination of good planning, self-awareness, and positive habits keeps you going toward your chosen direction, even if the path has ups and downs.

Chapter 20: Bringing It All Together

You have explored many sides of decision-making: from understanding what shapes your choices to dealing with sudden changes, from forming routines and staying flexible to coping with doubts and keeping motivation high. At this point, it is useful to see how these pieces fit together into a single process. This final chapter highlights how each element can help you move from feeling stuck to feeling sure of the steps you take. By weaving together what you have learned, you can become more skilled at deciding what you really want, seeing obstacles, and picking actions that suit you.

Recapping the Main Points
Before combining the parts, let us list the big lessons from earlier chapters:

- **Know Yourself**: Understand your values, emotions, and experiences that guide you.
- **Spot Common Obstacles**: Be aware of traps like overconfidence, social pressure, or fear.
- **Use Tools**: Checklists, pros and cons, mind maps, or scenario planning for clarity.
- **Stay Flexible**: Allow for changes in plans without losing sight of your main goals.
- **Manage Emotions Wisely**: Recognize how feelings can help or hinder your choices.
- **Face Uncertainty**: Accept that you might not have all facts, but you can move forward responsibly.
- **Keep up Motivation**: Link tasks to your personal "why" and give yourself small boosts along the way.
- **Reflect and Learn**: Review outcomes to see what worked or did not, then adjust in the future.

Each of these threads contributes to a strong decision-making style that responds to real-life complexities. When combined, they form a pattern for both everyday tasks (such as deciding how to spend a Saturday) and large-scale decisions (like choosing a career or moving to a new place).

- **The Flow of a Good Decision**
  You can think of a good decision-making process as having these phases:
- **Identify What Is at Stake**: What choice needs to be made, and why does it matter?
- **Gather Facts and Feelings**: Collect relevant info, but also check your emotions and values.
- **Brainstorm or Compare Options**: Use a method like pros and cons, a decision tree, or discussions with others.
- **Check for Obstacles and Risks**: See if fear, social pressure, or other traps are swaying you.
- **Decide on a Path**: Make a choice once you have enough clarity—not perfect clarity, but sufficient to feel reasonably confident.
- **Take Action**: Implement your choice. Break it into tasks if it is large, form routines to carry it out, and manage your motivation.
- **Stay Flexible**: Watch for signs that you might need to adjust. Be willing to shift if new info appears.
- **Review the Outcome**: After results appear, reflect on what went well or poorly. Use that insight next time.

This cycle can be repeated whenever a fresh decision arises. Over time, each round of decisions and reflections boosts your knowledge about yourself and the world.

Blending Facts with Personal Insight

One key theme is the balance between logic (facts, data) and personal insight (values, gut feelings). Decisions that ignore data can be naive. But decisions that ignore your heart can feel empty or unfulfilling. By blending the two, you make choices that feel both rational and right for your life. For example, if the data says a certain job pays well but your heart says you will not be happy in that environment, you might reconsider or look for a middle ground.

In practice, this blending can look like listing the pros and cons for each option, then seeing how you feel about the top two. If you notice strong excitement or dread, that can point to deeper preferences. Or if your feelings push you strongly toward an option, you still check facts to see if it is feasible. This harmony keeps you from being swayed only by emotion or by pure statistics.

Using Routines to Simplify Small Decisions

One way to reserve mental energy for bigger decisions is to reduce the clutter of small daily choices. Routines handle many everyday actions—when to wake up, when to check messages, when to do a daily task—so you do not waste your decision power on them each time. This leaves you more mental space for the choices that genuinely need careful thought.

If you find you are still overwhelmed by daily tasks, revisit your routine. Add or remove elements as needed. For instance, a consistent bedtime can enhance your energy the next day, which in turn sharpens your mind for decisions about work or family. A lunch routine might free up your lunch break for reading or taking a quick walk that refreshes you for afternoon decisions.

Handling Sudden Turns and Complicated Factors

Large or complex situations may involve multiple people, uncertain outcomes, or big consequences. Then, you might need to:

- **Gather Balanced Info**: Talk to various stakeholders, read different sources, and see every angle.
- **Map the Possible Outcomes**: Use scenario thinking to see what might happen if you choose A, B, or C.
- **Consider Others' Needs**: Check if your choice affects partners, kids, coworkers, or friends.
- **Make a Provisional Plan**: Choose a path but stay ready to pivot if things shift unexpectedly.

Staying flexible is crucial here. You do not want to keep flipping choices nonstop, but you also do not want to remain locked onto a sinking ship. The skill lies in watching for valid reasons to change course and ignoring minor bumps that do not truly warrant scrapping your plan.

Facing the Emotional Side

Emotions are not just random feelings; they often signal what matters to you. Fear can warn of real dangers, excitement can show a path you genuinely care about, anger might indicate something is unfair or crossing your boundaries. By observing these emotions calmly, you gather hints about your deeper wants. If you hide or deny your emotions, they might appear in unhelpful ways like procrastination or stress.

Yet, you do not want to let emotions rule unchallenged. Fact-checking your fear or excitement prevents you from jumping to extremes. For instance, if you feel a surge of excitement about a fast business pitch, you can still investigate whether the pitch is realistic. If your fear says, "This is risky," you can gather data to see how big the risk actually is. Emotions point the way, and facts confirm if the path is sound.

Motivation as a Driving Force

Without motivation, even clear decisions can stall. That is why you keep your "why" in mind—the personal connection that energizes your effort. By setting up small rewards, sharing progress with supportive friends, and noting small wins, you maintain momentum. When motivation dips, check if you are tired or if your plan needs adjusting. Sometimes, all you need is a slight tweak to your routine or a day's rest to reignite your spark.

Remember, long-term motivation is often about internal reasons rather than external prizes. You might start a project for the paycheck, but to keep going over months or years, it helps to find a sense of personal meaning. Ask yourself how the project aligns with your interests or what you can learn from it that you genuinely value.

Reviewing and Learning from Each Outcome

An important piece of becoming better at decisions is reviewing what happens afterward. This involves two steps:

- **Immediate Look**: Right after you see results, note if you met your target or not. Did your approach work as planned, or did you hit unexpected snags? This fresh viewpoint captures details that fade with time.
- **Calmer Reflection Later**: Wait a bit for any strong emotions to settle, then do a more thoughtful review. You might realize certain factors were out of your control, or you might spot a repeated pattern in your handling of projects.

These reviews reduce the chance of making the same mistake again. They also let you replicate what worked well. Over time, your decision-making process becomes more refined because you keep integrating lessons from each past choice.

Confidence Grows from Practice

If you often feel stuck or uncertain, remember that confidence in decision-making is built through practice, not from reading alone. Each time you go through the steps—identify a need, gather info, weigh options, choose, and review—you gain a bit more trust in your ability. Even if you fail sometimes, you learn how to adjust. Over many decisions, you start seeing patterns in what helps or hinders you.

Confidence also comes from realizing that no decision is final. You can often adjust, pivot, or correct course if needed. This knowledge can soothe the fear that one wrong choice will ruin everything. Very few decisions are truly irreversible. Most allow you some room to fix errors or find a new route.

Staying Alert for Rigid or Extreme Thinking

As you move forward, keep an eye out for the return of common traps. You might slip back into overconfidence, ignoring early warnings. Or you might become too rigid, refusing to adapt a plan that is clearly failing. Or you could let peer pressure steer you into choices you do not really want. Periodically remind yourself of these pitfalls so you catch them early.

Some ways to spot them include:

- **Journaling**: Write down your thoughts once a week. If you see repeated patterns of "I know best," or "I do not care what anyone else thinks," that might be a sign of overconfidence or ignoring social input.
- **Accountability Partners**: Have a friend or colleague who can nudge you if they see you slipping into old habits. For example, "Hey, are you sure you are not ignoring the negative feedback again?"
- **Short Checklists**: Create a personal checklist that reminds you to question social pressure, re-check assumptions, or confirm you are not missing simpler options.

Balancing Big Dreams with Practical Steps
Some decisions relate to ambitious goals like launching a business, becoming highly skilled in a field, or improving a community. Ambition is great, but it must be matched with practical steps. Large dreams can seem far off; that can breed discouragement if you do not see results quickly. This is where short-term milestones come in. You can aim for the stars yet still move in small, logical increments, measuring your progress as you go.

Staying practical also means facing real-world constraints: finances, time, location, or responsibilities to others. Balancing big dreams with these details is not about giving up. It is about planning realistically so your dream has a real chance of success.

Adapting the Approach for Different Areas of Life
Decision-making is not just about work or school. You can apply the same process to personal matters like health, friendships, and hobbies. For instance, deciding how to handle conflicts with friends uses similar skills: understanding the situation, seeing each person's perspective, staying open to compromise, and reflecting afterward on what worked to rebuild trust.

By using a consistent decision framework across various parts of your life, you build a habit of thorough, thoughtful choices. This consistency also makes it easier to notice when you rush or skip steps, because you will feel the difference.

Accepting Partial Unknowns
Even the best planning will not remove all uncertainty. Some decisions involve future trends or other people's actions you cannot control. Rather than seeing this as an error, accept it as part of the process. You do your best with the knowledge at hand, remain flexible, and trust your ability to respond if the situation changes. This acceptance can reduce stress and let you focus on what you can do, not on the impossible task of predicting everything.

Encouraging Personal Growth Through Decisions
Each choice you face is a chance to grow in understanding your strengths, your weaknesses, and your preferences. You discover what style of learning suits you, how you handle pressure, or what you really value in a job or relationship. By looking at decisions as learning experiences rather than pass/fail tests, you gain personal growth no matter how the result turns out.

Over years, you might find that your decision skills have led you to new places—new jobs, new friendships, new perspectives. These changes often come not from a single huge choice but from a chain of smaller, well-managed ones.

Building on Others' Advice Without Losing Your Voice
It is wise to talk to experts or mentors when tackling complex issues. They can share knowledge you lack. However, remember that their advice is just one input among many. You must still make the final call based on your situation. If a mentor says, "You must do X to succeed," but it clashes with your personal values or resources, reflect carefully before following it blindly. The best outcomes come from weaving outside opinions with your own insight.

Recognizing Progress
When you make strides—big or small—it is good to pause and note the achievement. This does not have to be elaborate. A simple acknowledgment like "I reached a milestone" or "I finished that tricky part" can lift your spirits. If you have family, friends, or a group that supported you, share the news with them. This recognition keeps you excited about pressing on, especially if there is more to do.

If you skip these moments of recognition, your progress might feel invisible. Then you risk losing the drive to keep going, because it seems like all effort and no payoff. Even if you do not want a formal reward, a little pat on your own back can help.

Sharing What You Learned
A powerful way to lock in your own knowledge is to teach or share it with

someone else. If you successfully navigate a tough decision—like picking a study path or learning a new skill—try explaining your steps to a friend who is also curious. This helps you see how you did it, and you might discover areas you can refine. Also, you give them a blueprint they can adapt for their own use.

Passing on insights also builds a supportive community. When people share methods for better decisions, it raises the overall ability of families, workplaces, and friendships to handle challenges. Everyone benefits from a culture where thoughtful choices are the norm.

Handling the Rare Case of Very High Stakes

Most decisions allow for changes if things go wrong. But a few—like a major surgery choice or signing a binding legal agreement—may have long-term effects that are hard to undo. In these cases, you want to be extra thorough. You might consult more experts, take more time, or do deeper checks. You still cannot guarantee a perfect outcome, but you can reduce the chance of a major regret by being diligent.

Even then, if you realize later there was a better route, try to focus on what you learned rather than living in regret. You made the best decision you could with the info you had. Dwelling on past errors without pulling lessons from them only adds to stress. Instead, accept that some calls are truly tough and carry heavy consequences; we do our best, then move forward.

Noticing Your Own Transformation

As you apply these principles—knowing yourself, staying flexible, using tools, and so on—you might sense a shift in how you handle daily life. Maybe you feel less stressed about small uncertainties. Maybe you speak up more in group decisions. Maybe you weigh pros and cons more naturally instead of acting on impulse. These changes are signs that your approach to decision-making is maturing.

At times, you might slip back into old habits. That is normal. Recognize it when it happens, take a breath, and remind yourself of the methods you have learned. Overcoming entrenched patterns might take repeated effort. Each slip is a chance to practice again and further embed the new mindset.

Carrying This Skill Forward
Decision-making is not a one-time ability you learn and are done with. It is an ongoing skill that grows throughout your life. As new technologies, social shifts, and personal situations arise, you will find fresh angles to consider. Keep your mind open, adapt the frameworks you have learned, and continue reflecting on what works. In that way, your decision-making becomes an evolving art, always being refined by your growing experience.

By piecing everything together—recognizing your personal drivers, using practical tools, handling emotions, respecting uncertainty, staying motivated, and learning from outcomes—you have a full toolkit to move from stuck to certain. While you will still face moments of doubt, you now have methods to see through the confusion. You can test options, pivot when needed, trust your core values, and keep a healthy rhythm of self-review.

Final Thoughts
Bringing it all together means you see decision-making as a cycle of planning, acting, reviewing, and adjusting. You do not demand perfection from yourself, and you do not hide from uncertain situations. You acknowledge that each step forward can teach you something new. By being patient, aware, and ready to adapt, you forge a path that fits who you are while still meeting the challenges of the world.

This holistic approach transforms decision-making from a source of anxiety to a method of growth. You become less stuck because you have reliable ways to clarify confusion and commit to choices that feel right. You become more certain not because you magically know the future, but because you trust your process, your ability to learn, and your willingness to adapt. In the end, that is what allows you to handle life's many options with calm and confidence, stepping forward into each new day with your eyes open to possibility.

www.ingramcontent.com/pod-product-compliance
Lightning Source LLC
LaVergne TN
LVHW012107070526
838202LV00056B/5648